Ghosts

of the

Wild West

Dedication:
To the ghosts that haunt us and give us a reason to pull the past into the present. We hope that we've done your stories justice.

Content Warning: This book contains retellings of historical events. Some events include references to suicide, murder, and gruesome accidents and may not be appropriate for all audiences.

Cover design by Jonathan Norberg
Text design by Karla Linder
Edited by Jenna Barron
Proofread by Emily Beaumont
All images copyrighted.
Shelley Anderson: 132; **Brianna Royle Koqka:** 133
Images used under license from Shutterstock.com:
Covers and silhouettes: **Croisy:** snake; **DianaFinch:** skull
Interior: **breakermaximus:** 31; **Daniel Eskridge:** 1; **KiHinko:** 75; **Lario Tus:** 49

10 9 8 7 6 5 4 3 2 1

Ghosts of the Wild West: Stories from Deadwood, Tombstone, and the Old Frontier

Published by Adventure Publications
An imprint of AdventureKEEN
310 Garfield Street South
Cambridge, Minnesota 55008
(800) 678-7006
www.adventurepublications.net
Printed in the USA
LCCN 2025022858 (print); 2025022859 (ebook)
ISBN 978-1-64755-545-0 (pbk.); 978-1-64755-546-7 (ebook)

Acknowledgments

The authors would like to thank several people who made this book possible:

Our families for putting up with us when we retreat into a writing cave.

All of the members of our publishing team at AdventureKEEN, who've given our stories a home.

Our agent, Dawn Frederick at Red Sofa Literary, who keeps us on track.

The keepers of haunted places, who embrace the weirdness that comes with being caretakers of a special kind of history.

The witnesses who've shared their experiences. Sometimes telling others what you've experienced is scarier than seeing a ghost because you never know how people will react. We believe you.

And last but not least, the ghosts themselves—for your persistence in reaching through the ether to share your stories. We are honored to help you tell them.

Important Note

Curiosity sometimes leads people to go out looking for ghosts and monsters, but please respect the law, as well as the rights and privacy of others.

Most importantly, we ask anyone who investigates the paranormal to exhibit extreme caution. Do not take this lightly. Tragically, people have died while pursuing legends. Your life is precious, and it is not worth risking. If there is any danger, please, let the legends remain as legends.

Furthermore, the information provided in this book is for reading entertainment purposes only. The authors and publisher do not assume and hereby disclaim any liability to any party for any loss, damage, or disruption caused by any other use of this information.

Preface

The ghosts of the Wild West are some of the most notorious and lively spirits. They are legends, larger than life. Some of these ghosts even have songs named after them, like Belle Starr and Jesse James.

The Wild West was a time of loose morals and vigilante justice. Hangings were a spectacle, worthy of a price for admission. On some occasions, a sentence for a crime could get creative, like a grave robber's banishment to a deserted island to fend for himself in the wilderness. Constitutional concepts like "innocent until proven guilty" and the right to a humane execution hadn't yet been born, as evidenced by Tom Ketchum's accidental decapitation for the crime of robbing a train.

The slightest glimmer of hope in the form of a gold nugget could set off a mad rush. For a lucky few, fortune would change overnight. For many others, dreams would be crushed under boulders of greed, and lives would be lost thanks to rampant lawlessness.

It was a time when robbing graves or stealing payroll from a train were career choices, as was turning tricks or running a brothel. It was a time when desperation ran thick—and, sometimes, the only choice was to kill or be killed.

The Pinkerton Detectives, an agency founded by Allan Pinkerton, was born. Although private, it was the country's first attempt at unified law enforcement. However, a botched raid that left Jesse James's mother with one arm did nothing to help their cause.

Outlaws were often on the run, and good men were killed chasing after them. It makes sense that the spirits of both would be restless. These unsettled souls sometimes make their presence known in more than one regular haunt.

Tracking them down and telling their stories wasn't always easy. Then again, nothing about the Wild West ever was.

—Jessica Freeburg and Natalie Fowler

Outlaws & Sharp-shooters

Tom "Black Jack" Ketchum

Philmont Scout Ranch
(Cimarron, New Mexico)

The youngest of eight children, Thomas Edward "Black Jack" Ketchum was born on October 31, 1863, in San Saba County, Texas. Tom's mother died when he was only 10. As he got older, Tom and his older brother, Sam, worked as cowboys on ranches in western Texas and eastern New Mexico.

In 1892, Tom and Sam banded together with a group of outlaws that robbed a train near Nutt, New Mexico, that was carrying $20,000 in payroll. In 1895, Tom and his group killed a man in what Tom later admitted was murder for hire.

On June 10, 1896, Tom and Sam robbed a store and post office in Liberty, New Mexico. They were chased out of town by a posse, and they escaped after a gunfight left most of the posse dead.

On September 3, 1897, the Ketchum gang robbed another train and reaped $20,000 in gold and $40,000 in silver. Afterward, they hid in a cave near Folsom, New Mexico.

On July 11, 1899, Tom's gang robbed a train without him, and his brother Sam was severely wounded. Two weeks later, on July 24, Sam died from gangrene in the Santa Fe Penitentiary.

Not knowing that his brother had died, Tom attempted to rob a train alone on August 16, 1899. The conductor, who was being held up for the third time, was ready. He shot Tom in the right elbow, causing him to fall backward off the train. At the next stop, the conductor alerted authorities.

Badly injured, Tom was arrested the next day; his arm had to be amputated. He was transferred to Clayton, where he was sentenced to death by hanging.

After hearing that Tom's gang would attempt to free him, his hanging was expedited. On April 26, 1901, the event was a spectacle. People came from all over to watch the outlaw die, and tickets to the ghastly event were sold.

Unfortunately, the hangmen forgot to remove the 200-pound sandbag that they had used to test the rope. As Tom fell through the trap, the additional weight was enough to decapitate him. Thankfully, the hood over his head was pinned to his shirt, or his head would have rolled into the crowd.

Black Jack Ketchum was the only person to be put to death for robbing a train and, at that point, the only person in the US who was decapitated during a hanging. In the years that followed, a death sentence for train robbery was declared unconstitutional.

Philmont Scout Ranch
(Cimarron, New Mexico)
Summer 1963

Skip hiked along with his fellow scouts, taking in the beauty of the mountains that rose around them. For about the millionth time that week, he felt lucky to be on this scouting trip of a lifetime.

Yesterday, they saw an abandoned goldmine. Today, the scouts were hiking to see one of Black Jack Ketchum's cave hideouts. Skip was hopeful that their leader would let them set up camp there. He wanted to sleep under the stars in the same place the outlaws did.

By late afternoon, the troop reached the cave, which was actually more of an overhang created by a large rock that jutted out from the side of the mountain. The boys dropped their gear in a pile and spread out to explore.

Skip made his way to their scoutmaster. "Could we set up camp here tonight?"

Billy added, "That would be amazing. Can we?"

The scoutmaster shook his head. "Sorry, boys, scout rules say we can only camp at official sites."

Later, back on the trail, Skip trudged along, disappointed and tired from the day's adventure. Billy tugged his arm and held him back, while other scouts passed by them.

"I've got an idea," whispered Billy.

Skip glanced sideways at Billy and waited. Billy had four older brothers, so his ideas were usually pretty good.

"Let's set up our tents away from Mr. Party Pooper.

Skip chuckled. They had started calling their troop leader Mr. Party Pooper about an hour into their first day, when he stopped them from jumping into a creek.

"And then," continued Billy, "we can sneak out with our sleeping bags and come back here."

Skip glanced back to see how far they'd come from the hideout. The trail was easy, and depending upon how far away the campsite was, it wouldn't be difficult to find their way back.

When the campsite appeared just around the next bend, the matter was decided. After more whispered discussions, they invited Steven, Andy, and Kevin to join them. The five boys strategically pitched their tents as far away from Mr. Party Pooper as possible, which turned out to be a comfortable distance of several hundred feet.

By 11 p.m., the rest of the scouts and their fearless leader were sound asleep. The five boys snuck out of their tents with their sleeping bags and made their way back to the outlaw hideout.

"Let's build a fire," Skip said.

The others agreed, and soon they had a small fire going.

"I can't believe we're going to sleep where Black Jack Ketchum hid with his crew," Kevin said.

"I can't believe his head fell off when they hanged him," Billy noted.

Skip thought about that with a shiver.

"Do you think they killed anyone right here?" asked Andy.

"Nah," said Skip, "they only killed the posse members that were chasing them, and the posse never found this place."

After the fire burned down and the adrenaline from sneaking away from camp wore off, the boys settled into their sleeping bags.

As Skip was drifting toward sleep, he heard a scuffle in the bushes. Startled awake, he realized that he was paralyzed. He tried to shout but couldn't.

A cowboy darted out of the bushes and ran toward the overhang. The man was dressed in black. Parts of him seemed solid, but other parts seemed translucent. His hat was tattered, and his teeth were yellow. His beard was overgrown, and his face was red and sweaty. He held a revolver in his hand.

Gunfire thundered nearby. The cowboy fired six shots into the trees and ran to stand next to Skip, oblivious to the boy in the sleeping bag. He discharged the shell casings from his revolver, and they fell onto Skip's sleeping bag.

As the gunslinger reloaded and fired more shots into the trees, he seemed to notice Skip for the first time. Surprise registered on his face. "You're not supposed to be here," he growled and then disappeared into thin air.

Somehow, Skip eventually managed to fall asleep.

The next morning, he awoke after his friends shook him out of a sound slumber. The night's events slowly came back to him, and he told his buddies about his crazy dream.

As he started to roll up his sleeping bag, six shell casings tumbled out of his bedding. He gathered them and shoved them into his pocket.

* * *

When Skip returned home, he and his father took the shell casings to a local gun expert. The expert dated the shells to approximately 1878 but remarked about their like-new condition. He also noted that they still smelled like gunpowder.

For the rest of his life, Skip often wondered about his ghostly encounter and the gift he'd been given by Black Jack Ketchum. He knew what he saw, but his mind struggled to make sense of how it could've happened. Nevertheless, six gun casings had, quite literally, landed in his lap. He would be forever grateful.

Jesse James

Talbott Tavern
(Bardstown, Kentucky)
Family Farm (Kearney, Missouri)

Jesse James was born on September 5, 1847. His parents were slave owners who ran a hemp farm in Kearney, Missouri. When Jesse was young, his father headed to California in search of gold, leaving Jesse's mother to run the farm and raise the children. While there, he died of an illness. Jesse's mother remarried.

When the Civil War broke out, the family proudly supported the Confederate Army. Jesse's older brother, Frank, joined a Confederate group of guerilla fighters who planned attacks on Union militiamen.

In 1863, the farm was invaded by Union militiamen out looking for information. They beat and whipped 16-year-old Jesse and tortured his stepfather, wanting information about guerilla fighters.

After this traumatic experience, despite his young age, Jesse joined a guerrilla group himself. Led by "Bloody Bill" Anderson, Jesse acted as an enthusiastic participant in the Centralia Massacre, which began with the killing of at least 22 unarmed Union soldiers on leave and ended with more than 100 other Union soldiers being brutally murdered, scalped, and mutilated.

After the Civil War, Jesse was embittered by the Confederate loss. He and Frank wanted to continue the fight. They did so by targeting a bank that was said to be owned by the man who had killed Jesse's hero, Bloody Bill. The brothers rode into Gallatin, Missouri, and, in broad daylight, shot an unarmed cashier and stole what turned out to be worthless paper.

Eventually, Frank and Jesse joined forces with Cole Younger, another former Confederate guerrilla soldier. They became known as the James-Younger Gang, which later became the James Gang. Jesse craved the spotlight. He wrote letters to newspaper editor (and former Confederate soldier) John Newman Edwards, who published his statements and fueled his ego.

In the 1870s, the James Gang thrived—stealing from stagecoaches and robbing banks and trains with no recourse, in part because of the support of Confederate sympathizers.

In September 1876, the James Gang finally ran out of luck in Northfield, Minnesota. The townspeople had no patience for the outlaw, who was trying to make himself look like Robin Hood, hundreds of miles from his home territory. Two of the James Gang were shot on sight. The rest were hunted down and killed. The only ones to escape were Frank and Jesse. They were forced into hiding, which was difficult for Jesse's restless soul and unquenchable craving for attention.

By 1879, he returned to his life of crime. In 1881, the Governor of Missouri posted a $10,000 reward for the delivery of Jesse James—dead or alive. Jesse was shot in the back of the head by Bob Ford, a member of his own gang.

Bob and Charlie Ford were tried before a jury and convicted for the murder. However, they were immediately pardoned by the governor for their crime.

Jesse James died with few friends. Yet, as the years passed, his legend grew exponentially. His escapades, as they are retold, overshadow the fact that his murderous and bloodthirsty lifestyle was the fuel that satisfied his desperate need for attention—perhaps giving him in death what he never could obtain in life. No wonder his spirit is restless and said to be haunting two locations.

* * *

The Old Talbott Tavern and Inn (Bardstown, Kentucky)

Jesse James was one of the most famous guests ever to stay at the Old Talbott Tavern and Inn, in what is now Bardstown, Kentucky. (When the hotel was built, the town was part of Virginia.)

After a night of drinking and playing cards, Jesse was asleep in his favorite room on the second floor, a room adorned with a mural of flying birds. He woke in the middle of the night in the throes of a night terror. He grabbed his gun and shot at the wall. Later, he admitted that, when he awoke, he thought the birds had come alive and were attacking him. The bullet holes were never repaired and are still visible in the wall.

Spring 2018

Elizabeth closed the ledger and sighed. It had been a long day, and she wasn't sad to sit in the quiet. Her senses stood at attention when she heard footsteps walking above her. Knowing that the rooms were vacant, she should have felt afraid. But working in the haunted hotel had made her accustomed to things like footless footsteps and the sounds of doors slamming unexpectedly and for no reason. The sounds disappeared down the hall, and she went back to her tasks.

She flipped off the light at the front desk and gathered the envelopes with the day's cash receipts from the inn and tavern. Just as she started for the stairs that led up to the office safe, Colby, the cook, banged through the door from the bar.

"Oh, my goodness!" Elizabeth exclaimed, startled.

Colby grinned. "Sorry about that. I didn't mean to frighten you."

"It's fine. I heard footsteps a few minutes ago, so I was already on edge."

Their attention was diverted when they caught movement on the landing above. A man in a long coat disappeared down the hall. They looked at each other.

"No one has checked in for the night, right?" asked Colby.

"It's entirely vacant."

In silent agreement, they headed up the stairs to pursue what they knew was probably a ghost. Together, they followed the figure down the hall and watched as he disappeared through the door to the fire escape.

Colby opened the door, assuming the figure had climbed down the fire escape. Instead, it remained on the landing.

Elizabeth gasped as the ghost locked eyes with her and laughed. It was a manic, hideous laugh.

Then, suddenly, the figure vanished and was gone.

* * *

Just a few weeks later, as Elizabeth watched a documentary on television, an image flashed upon the screen. The narrator spoke about Jesse James.

Elizabeth grabbed her husband's arm. "That's the ghost I saw the other night."

From that moment on, the people at the Old Talbott Tavern and Inn knew they had a special guest from the afterlife: Jesse James.

* * *

The Family Farm (Kearney, Missouri)

Jesse James's childhood farm is also reportedly haunted. After he rose to notoriety, the Pinkerton Detectives visited there, an attempt to capture Jesse and Frank. Throwing a bomb through the window, they killed his stepbrother; his mother's right arm had to be amputated at the elbow because of shrapnel injuries. Frank and Jesse were not anywhere near the property at the time of the attack.

After Jesse was killed, he was buried at the family farm, where his mother could guard his body from curious thrill seekers. It was later exhumed and reburied at Kearney's Mount Olivet Cemetery.

Today, the farm is a museum. Visitors report unexplained lights moving inside and outside the house. The sound of galloping horses and gunshots are often heard on the grounds. Staff have also reported feeling uneasy inside the home, as if watched by an intense presence—leaving them to wonder if the outlaw's spirit lingers.

It's no wonder this place is haunted. Twice, it was the scene of great violence and terror. The residual fear from those events could embed within the ether, influencing the energy there for decades to follow.

Tom Horn

Wrangler Western Store
(Cheyenne, Wyoming)
Columbia Cemetery
(Boulder, Colorado)

I n the late 1800s, a grassroots, guerilla-style war was emerging on the open range of Wyoming. Battles between cattle barons and homesteaders would later become known as the Johnson County War.

The cattle barons owned large herds, sometimes numbering in the thousands, that grazed in the open range. The homesteaders, who legally owned land on the range, raised much smaller herds, mostly for their own families. However, their homesteads were right in the middle of the cattle barons' grazing lands. The homesteaders wanted the cattle barons to move off their land, and the cattle barons wanted the homesteaders to do the same.

In April 1892, the cattle barons hired 23 sharpshooters to kill a list of 70 homesteaders. When those sharpshooters arrived by train near Casper, Wyoming, a man named Tom Horn was among them. Tom had served as a scout with the US Cavalry at the age of 16. In 1890, he was employed by the Pinkerton Detective Agency; its specialty was tracking down suspected lawbreakers. However, Tom had lost his job because, quite often, instead of bringing his targets back to the courts, he would simply take matters into his own hands. Now, he had a chance to become an "enforcer" for the cattle barons, tasked with "dealing justice" to targets who'd been accused of stealing cattle or taking away grazing lands. Tom quickly gained a reputation—due, in part, to his habit of bragging about the number of men he killed.

On July 18, 1901, Tom's target was Kelsey P. Nickell, a retired US Cavalryman who had homesteaded a ranch with his wife, Mary, at Iron Mountain in Wyoming. Tom had been tracking Kelsey for a while. He could recognize the horse Kelsey rode, as well as the coat and hat Kelsey typically wore. When Tom saw Kelsey ride up the road toward his family's home, he set about to finish his job. Tragically, Tom's bullets tore through the body of Kelsey's 14-year-old son, Willie, who'd run an errand wearing his father's coat and hat.

* * *

Cheyenne, Wyoming
January 1902

Tom Horn sat down with Marshal Joe LeFors in the sheriff's office, located across from the bar. Joe knew that Tom wouldn't be able to resist a job offer . . . or a chance to brag about his "accomplishments." That's why a deputy sheriff and a court stenographer were hiding in the next room, writing down every word.

"I'm looking for someone willing to take matters into their own hands when necessary," said Joe.

Tom nodded. "That's no problem here."

The men continued talking. Tom lit up when Joe asked about the range wars and Iron Mountain.

"Have you got your money yet for the killing of Kelsey?" asked Joe.

"I got that before I did the job," Tom replied. "Killing men is my specialty. I look at it as a business proposition, and I think I have the corner on the market."

Tom was arrested the next morning. On October 12, 1903, he was convicted of murder in the first degree for Willie Nickell's shooting. On November 20, Tom Horn was hanged. It took him 17 minutes to die.

* * *

Not long after Tom's execution, inmates of the county jail where Tom spent his final days reported hearing strange sounds. They attributed the eerie noises to the ghost of the hanged assassin. People throughout the community reported seeing the ghostly apparitions of Tom Horn and his young victim, Willie Nickell.

In recent years, several people have reported seeing a ghostly cowboy in the Wrangler Western Store—a historic, three-story building that was built in Cheyenne in 1882. Many assume the ghost is that of Tom Horn, wandering throughout the building, sparking fear in patrons and sales associates.

* * *

Columbia Cemetery (Boulder, Colorado) October 2024

"Found it!" Isabelle shouted enthusiastically. She stood over the gravestone, her flashlight shining on the red-tone slab.

"In loving memory of Tom Horn, 1861 to 1903," Ella read the inscription.

"His body is right beneath our feet," Brie said with a shudder.

The girls exchanged glances and took a step to the side.

"Now we're standing on top of Charles Horn," Brie said, shaking her head.

"Tom's buried right beside his brother and sister-in-law," Ella noted, resigned to the fact that there was no place to stand that wasn't on top of a corpse.

A breeze rustled a tree, causing orange and yellow leaves to softly rain onto a nearby tombstone. The branch of the large pine that hung over Tom Horn's grave swayed as long shadows, created by the girls' flashlights, seemed to slither across the yellowed grass.

"I don't like it out here," Brie said, a quiver breaking the last word.

"I know, it's creepy," Ella said, putting an arm around her sister's shoulders. "We won't stay long."

They'd come to the graveyard on a mission: to see if the legends were true.

Isabelle pulled a notebook from her backpack and held up her notes. "Joe Nickell was Willie's third cousin twice removed. He was also a paranormal investigator and researcher. I found an article he wrote about his cousin's murder. It said that he came to this graveyard in 1998 to see for himself if the ghost of Tom Horn was here—and that he danced on his grave."

A light crack, like a twig snapping, pulled the girls' attention toward a tall tree. Its branches had all but given up the fight to keep their leaves. The branches stretched out from the trunk like lanky arms trying to touch some faraway object.

"What was that?" Ella whispered.

"It was probably just an animal, like a rabbit or a squirrel," Isabelle replied with more optimism than she actually felt.

"They say that Tom Horn's ghost can be seen swinging from a noose."

"Don't read anymore," Brie whined. "This is too scary. I want to go."

The dry leaves that had fallen to the ground rustled, as if something scuffled through them.

"It could be a big animal—like a mountain lion or a bear," Ella said.

"Or worse, a weird person who likes to hang out in cemeteries at night," Brie added.

The girls took one last look at Tom's gravestone. Brie pulled something small from her pocket and set it on the base of the stone: a plastic cowboy holding a rifle, similar to the tiny green army men found at dollar stores.

The girls walked quickly away from the grave. Another gust of wind shook more leaves off the trees. Brie looked back at the gravestone. Movement in the tall, bare tree caught her attention.

"Oh, my gosh," she whispered, grabbing Ella's arm.

Ella and Isabelle turned, and all three girls stared, frozen, for several seconds.

Looped around the largest branch was a rope. Hanging from a noose at the end of that rope was a man. His arms and legs swayed limply from his body. In the moonlight, he was only a dark silhouette.

Another twig snapped, and the girls screamed. They ran to their car, jumped inside, and locked the doors. As Ella started the car, the girls looked toward the tree.

The shadowy figure was gone.

A gust of wind sent leaves scattering across the road as Ella shifted the car into drive and sped away from the cemetery.

"We saw him," Brie said excitingly. "We saw Tom Horn's ghost!"

* * *

It's hard to know why or how the spirit of one man might haunt two places. But without the constraints of a physical body, it seems that a soul is no longer bound by space or time. In other words, it can go wherever it pleases. Does Tom Horn's soul wander the streets and stores of Cheyenne, where he was finally held responsible for murdering an innocent boy? Does he linger near his grave, tormented by his own execution? If the legends are true, it seems the answer to both questions is yes.

Jean Baptiste

Southern Shore of the Great Salt Lake

Fremont and Antelope Islands (Utah)

Some men of the Wild West sought their fortune in prospecting, and others established operations to support the great Western expansion. However, not all entrepreneurs followed lawful business pursuits. Although their actions stepped outside the bounds of the law, they aren't defined as "outlaws" by traditional Wild West standards. They were profiteers, and Jean Baptiste was one such man who sought gain in the most macabre fashion.

* * *

Salt Lake City, Utah
January 1862

Officer Henry Heath covered his nose with his handkerchief and looked at the dead body, lying on the slab at the morgue. The body of Moroni Clawson had been in the morgue for three days. His face was turning a strange, greenish-gray color and was starting to puff up.

Officer Heath had been summoned by the coroner to help figure out what to do next. No one from the man's family had come to claim him, and no one—least of all the coroner—wanted bodies in the morgue beyond three days. This one already had a stink, despite the cooler temperatures of January.

Moroni and his group of Mormon men had attacked the already retreating governor of the Utah Territory, John Dawson. Moroni had been shot by law enforcement after a standoff, and Officer Heath felt bad about that.

Governor Dawson hadn't even lasted a month in his post before being run off. Since the governor was already retreating, the boys hadn't needed to take it so far. But they were making a point about not wanting federal interference and must have been sending the governor back with a message. Officer Heath could respect that.

"We can't have him here, stinkin' up the place," the coroner said.

"I know," said Officer Heath. "I'll take care of it myself."

"What do you mean?"

"I'm going to send over my tailor. We will get him a nice suit and get him buried in the ground all good and proper. I'll see to it that it happens by tomorrow."

The coroner nodded. "That's right nice of you."

"It's the least I can do."

"Just make it quick," said the coroner.

With a nod of his head, Officer Heath went to see about the preparations.

* * *

A week later, Officer Heath returned to the police station after a long day. When he arrived, a gentleman was talking to the officer behind the desk.

"Here he is now," said the officer.

The man stretched out his hand. "I'm Moroni Clawson's brother. I understand you took care of burying him."

Officer Heath took off his hat with one hand and shook the man's hand with his other. "Yes, sir."

"My family is grateful, but I've come to get him. We'd like him to be buried with his family in Dawson."

"Yes, sir, of course," said Officer Heath. "We can arrange that."

* * *

On the morning of the exhumation, Officer Heath was in his office when commotion erupted in the front of the building. He went to investigate.

"You!" Mr. Clawson pointed at him and shook his fist. His face was red. "You told me you took care of my brother. What kind of game are you playing?"

The officer at the front desk jumped up and held his hand at the ready, in case he needed to protect Officer Heath from an attack.

Officer Heath kept his voice calm. "I surely don't know what you're talking about, sir. What's happened?"

"My brother," the man sputtered, "you said you took care of him, buried him in a suit."

"Yes," said Officer Heath. "I did."

"Then why was he as naked as the day he was born? Not only that, he was lying face down! I've never seen such disrespect."

"I can assure you," said Officer Heath, growing angry himself, "I paid for his suit with my own money. It was tailored to fit him."

Both men fell silent.

Officer Heath began to realize the severity of what might have happened. "I buried that man in the ground myself," he said quietly. "He was wearing the suit that I bought for him. I saw it with my own eyes."

"It must have been stolen," said the other officer.

"I am going to find out by who," said Officer Heath.

* * *

Officer Heath started his investigation with the gravedigger, Jean Baptiste. He took some men with him to Jean's home, where they found his young wife, Dorothy Jennison. She informed them that her husband was working.

As the men turned to leave, one of the officers whispered, "Look." He pointed at a stack of boxes piled in the corner of the room. A dirty shirtsleeve was sticking out of one.

Officer Heath opened a box and took out a shirt. Bits of dirt fell to the ground at his feet. He poked around in the box and found a pair of shoes that could only fit a child. He also pulled out a large woman's dress, trimmed with lace. It was obvious that they had found who they were looking for, and if Officer Heath looked through all the boxes, he would probably find the missing suit.

The anger within him was soon replaced by horror and dread. He thought about his own daughter, Sarah, whom he had buried just nine months earlier. Feeling sick to his stomach, he dropped the large dress.

"Let's go," he said to the men.

They mounted their horses, and he led them to the Salt Lake City graveyard. They found Jean in the middle of the cemetery, digging a new grave.

"We need a word," said Officer Heath.

The man crawled out of the hole. "Yes, sir?"

"We've just come from your home, and we have some questions," said the lawman.

Understanding spread across the man's face, and he dropped to his knees. "Please, sir, don't kill me."

The officer yanked Jean to his feet. "Come with me."

Jean let himself be led along.

"That one?" Officer Heath asked, pointing at fresh, nearly frozen dirt that had recently been patted down.

Jean nodded slowly.

He yanked Jean by the arm. "That one?" he asked, pointing at another.

Jean nodded.

The pit in the lawman's stomach rose, and he wanted to vomit. He swallowed hard and continued. He pulled the thief from one grave to another, randomly pointing, but knowing exactly where he was going. Each time, Jean nodded.

Officer Heath discreetly slid his right hand to the worn leather holster that secured his pistol to his hip, and he felt for the cold, reassuring metal in his hand. He nodded with his head to Sarah's headstone.

"That one?" Officer Heath asked, careful to keep his voice steady.

Jean paused, and the officer held his breath, committed to killing the man if he gave the wrong answer.

Jean shook his head. "No."

Officer Heath's hand released his weapon. He marched Jean back to the others.

* * *

The town was collectively sickened by Jean Baptiste's disregard for the dead—he had robbed more than 300 graves. Burial clothes were very important to the community's Mormon faith. They believed they would be resurrected just as they were placed in their coffins. They couldn't very well have their loved ones ascending to the afterlife in their knickers or, worse, completely nude! Efforts were made to return the ill-gotten belongings to family members. The rest was eventually buried in a mass grave at the cemetery.

With citizens demanding justice, the Mormon leader Brigham Young noted that hanging would be too good for Jean Baptiste. No court records exist about what happened next.

"Grave Robber" was tattooed across Jean's forehead, and it was eventually decided that he would be exiled to Antelope Island. However, people realized that if it were a low-water year, Jean would be able to simply walk away. Therefore, it was instead decided that Fremont Island, a small cattle-grazing island off Antelope Island, would be a better destination.

* * *

Six weeks after he was banished, the herd's owners were there to check on their cattle. They found the dismantled remains of a small shed, which had been used to house provisions. One of the calves was dead, its hide cut into strips. Jean Baptiste was nowhere to be found and was never seen again. The owners suspected that he had fashioned a raft, using wood from the shed and leather from the hide, to make a daring escape.

* * *

Fielding Garr Ranch (Antelope Island, Utah) Summer 2024

Anna took one final walk through the ranch's rooms, even though she knew all the visitors were gone. She had personally walked the last family down the path and to the parking lot, answering their questions the whole way. They'd wanted to know more about Jean Baptiste.

Anna volunteered at the Fielding Garr Ranch on Antelope Island. As a history major on summer break, it was a perfect résumé builder. She would have done it even if her guidance counselor hadn't suggested it. She liked teaching other people about history.

Built in 1848 by Mormon pioneers, it had earned a place on the National Historic Registry as Utah's oldest working ranch. Fielding Garr had been a widower with nine children and was a member of the Church of Jesus Christ of Latter-day Saints—now known as the LDS Church. After Fielding's wife passed, the Church sent him to establish the ranch and gave him the job of managing the church's sheep and cattle on the island.

Today had been a busy day, and Anna appreciated the quiet. She could feel the walls trying to tell her their stories.

"Are you sure you're okay to finish alone?" Joan asked, handing her a stack of photocopies and folders.

They'd been tasked with putting together 100 informational packets for a fundraiser.

"I'm fine," she said, trying to keep her voice steady.

While Anna enjoyed being in the quiet house, she was not looking forward to being there alone. The surrounding forest—and basically the entire island—was rumored to be haunted.

"Okay," said Joan, "if you're sure."

Anna knew that Joan's elderly mother was in the hospital, and Joan was anxious to visit. "I'll be fine. I promise," said Anna, trying to make herself believe her own words.

Anna shooed her out the door. Then she locked it and sat down to work.

An hour later, with dusk very quickly turning into darkness, she stuffed the last set of papers into the last folder. She gathered her belongings, then stood at the front door for a moment, attempting to find courage to walk the path to the parking lot. Maybe she should radio the barn; people were still down there. But she didn't want to make anyone stop what they were doing just because she was afraid of ghosts.

Anna took a deep breath and set out for the path, trying not to think about the spirit of Jean Baptiste. Behind her, an owl hooted, and she jumped.

"Stop being a scaredy-cat," Anna whispered to herself. Yet she felt like she was being watched.

A twig snapped somewhere nearby, and shivers danced across the back of her neck. The hair on her arms stood at attention. She walked a little faster, knowing that the parking lot was almost in sight. The heaviness in the air wasn't just the humidity. It was a feeling: oppressive and sad.

As soon as she saw her car, she broke into a run. Anna clicked the key fob to unlock her car and, in a swift, single movement, slid into it.

Out of the corner of her eye, she saw a shadow move. She couldn't shake the feeling that someone was watching her, yet she reminded herself that she was safe and clicked the lock, just to be sure. She started the engine.

She pointed her car in the direction of the exit and drove faster than she should have to the causeway. As she neared the road to get her off the island, she saw it: A shadow rose along the shoreline, like a wisp of fog that morphed into something more—the unmistakable form of a man.

At first, she thought her mind was playing tricks on her, but then the shadow form began to move. It strode slowly along the edge, looking across the water.

She felt a sudden pang of sadness and a longing to reach the mainland, as if Jean Baptiste's spirit was making her feel what he felt so long ago, when he was banished to a life of solitude, separated from his family and friends.

Anna focused on the road ahead. As her wheels rumbled across the pavement, she glanced toward the shoreline again, but the man was gone. She decided that, from that moment on, she would only sign up for morning shifts.

* * *

Jean Baptiste reportedly haunts Antelope Island and Fremont Island. Plus, over the decades, witnesses reported seeing the apparition of a man wandering the southern shoreline of the Great Salt Lake—a soul trapped in an eternal loop of loneliness, seeking redemption for its sins.

Law &
Order

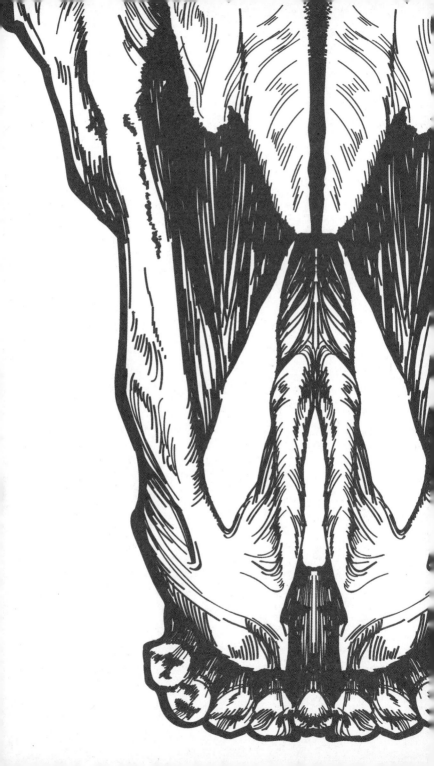

Wild Bill Hickok

**Wild Bill Bar
(Deadwood, South Dakota)
No. 10 Saloon
August 2, 1876**

The chips clanked into a pile on the table as the men took final assessments of their cards.

James Butler Hickok shifted in his seat and glanced over his shoulder. "You sure you won't change seats with me?"

"No, sir," Charles Rip replied, a hint of annoyance in his voice.

This wasn't the first time the legendary lawman, known throughout the country as Wild Bill, had asked Rip to let him have his seat. Wild Bill had a reputation for taking out unlawful men, and he knew he'd made more than a few enemies over the years. He didn't like sitting with his back to the door.

Wild Bill had spent several years serving in the Union Army as a sharpshooter and scout. That, coupled with his time as a lawman and marshal, made Wild Bill a legend. During his service, he racked up a number of killings, rumored at more than 100. His work as a lawman came to an end when he accidentally shot his deputy marshal—a tragedy that still haunted him. Now he made his way playing poker and even spent some time performing in Buffalo Bill Cody's popular Wild West show.

He drank a little too much these days, and his eyesight was getting progressively worse. But he'd married a woman he loved, Agnes, just a few months before coming to Deadwood. He arrived with Charles Utter's wagon train, along with a slew of prospectors, gamblers, sex workers, and Calamity Jane. He hoped to make enough money to send for Agnes and bring her here to be with him.

Captain Massie laid his cards on the table. His lips turned up slightly as he saw the others lay down their hands.

Wild Bill shook his head and said, "The old duffer, he broke me on the hand."

Before anyone at the table realized what was happening, a man walked up behind Wild Bill. A shot blasted from the barrel of his 45-caliber revolver, and the man screamed, "Damn you, take that!"

A slug ripped through Wild Bill's right cheek and hit Captain Massie in the wrist. Wild Bill's head lurched forward from the blast to the back of his skull. His body sat motionless in the chair for seconds that seemed like minutes—his eyes devoid of the spark of life that had shined from them only seconds ago.

His body slid to the floor with a sickening thud. His cards, which had fallen from his hands, lay spread on the table. Two black aces and two black eights would, from that day forward, be known as "the dead man's hand."

* * *

Wild Bill Bar, Fall 2010

"They say that one to two people were murdered a day in Deadwood. It was one of the deadliest towns in the history of the Wild West," said the tour guide.

From behind the bar, Leanne heard him lead a group of tourists into the room that sat on the spot where Wild Bill was believed to have been murdered. The actual bar, Nuttal & Mann's No. 10 Saloon, burned down—along with much of the rest of the town—just three years after Wild Bill's death. So the exact location of the infamous incident wasn't certain. But the resilient mining community had quickly rebuilt, this time with bricks instead of wood. Bars were erected where bars once stood. Hotels rose upon the ashes of old hotels. Brothels returned to the top floors, from one end of town to the other.

Leanne knew Wild Bill's story well. Jack McCall, disgruntled over Wild Bill winning all of his money the night before, sought revenge. As legend had it, Wild Bill gave Jack enough money back to cover his breakfast the next morning, but the gesture was received as an insult and only added to Jack's rage.

Leanne gazed toward the stairs that led to the bar's former brothel. She hated going up there. The energy always felt off: suffocating—that was the best way she could describe it.

She swallowed a lump in her throat. Leanne would have to venture up there before the end of her shift.

She'd been up there earlier that day to move some boxes, and she was sure her keys had fallen out of her pocket. She was also sure she'd seen a shadow figure move through the hallway toward her. She didn't know why, but it felt threatening.

Glancing out the front window, she saw the shadows growing longer in the street. She'd put off this chore as long as she could. If she didn't go now, it would be dark, which would make her expedition even creepier.

Clearing her throat, Leanne walked briskly toward the stairwell. "Just get it over with," she told herself.

The stairs groaned beneath her feet as she ascended them two at a time. Her heartbeat quickened as she peered down the hallway where she'd been moving boxes. A glint of silver caught her attention on the dusty, wooden planks.

She breathed a sigh of relief. "I'm just getting my keys, and then I'm getting out of here." She wasn't sure who she was talking to, but somehow it made her feel better to let them know what she was doing—so they'd leave her alone.

She rushed to the keys, scooped them up, and shoved them deep into her pocket as she kept an eye out for any movement. She saw it: a rush of black that crossed the hallway, from one room to another.

"Oh, no," she whispered, backing toward the steps, too afraid to take her eyes off the room into which the figure had just dashed.

She was just a few steps from the landing when something pushed her into the wall. Eyes wide with terror, Leanne opened her mouth to scream, but only a strangled squeak came out. She couldn't see any source of pressure, but something strong held her there, pressing her against the wall.

As abruptly as it began, the unseen presence released its grip, and Leanne's body fell away from the wall. Turning on her heels, she ran down the stairs, her feet barely keeping up with her body as she stumbled down the last few steps. She didn't stop running until she was behind the bar.

A man and woman sat at stools across from her, looking startled by her sudden appearance.

"Sorry," she said, catching her breath. "I didn't mean to scare you."

The woman furrowed her eyebrow. "You didn't," she replied, pointing behind Leanne. "We just watched an ashtray slide off that counter."

Leanne looked down. Sure enough, an ashtray lay upside down on the floor. She returned it to the counter. Thankfully, it had been empty.

"That actually happens a lot."

The woman's eyes lit up. "You mean, this bar is really haunted?"

"I think it's safe to say this entire town is haunted."

* * *

While the most prevalent spirit that haunts the Wild Bill Bar is something dark and angry—perhaps the energy of chaos left behind by such a traumatic murder or the spirit of the man responsible for it—many have reported seeing the ghost of Wild Bill himself. Some say he's still playing cards in the bar or walking down the streets of Deadwood, just as he did more than 100 years ago.

Seth Bullock

The Bullock Hotel
(Deadwood, South Dakota)

When Seth Bullock and Sol Star rolled into Deadwood, they had a simple plan: open a hardware store and sell their goods to local miners. The mining camp that had sprung up in a gulch of dead trees was growing with each wagon train that passed through the area. Men came from far and wide to stake their claim on a piece of the golden pie. Most of them walked away no richer than they walked in, but they'd risk it all to try.

Legends claim that Seth arrived in Deadwood within a day or two of Wild Bill Hickok's murder. Although many in the town reveled in its wildness, Deadwood was in desperate need of someone to usher in order.

Seth carried himself with an air of confidence that commanded respect. His tall stature, thick mustache, and steel-gray eyes made him an imposing figure. With experience as a sheriff in Montana, Seth was just the man to bring law to the notoriously lawless town.

Seth became a very highly respected figure in Deadwood. He and his team of deputies cleaned up the once-unruly town. The hardware store Seth and Sol established was a success. It survived the first fire that swept through Deadwood in 1879. Unfortunately, it was wiped out by a fire in 1894 that destroyed the lower business district. In its place, Seth erected a three-story, 64-room, luxury hotel with steam heat and bathrooms on each level. It was considered the height of luxury for its time.

For 25 years, Seth made sure his hotel ran smoothly, until his death from cancer in 1919. It seems that the man, once called the "finest type of frontiersman" by his friend Teddy Roosevelt, never really left his beloved hotel.

* * *

Bullock Hotel
Early 2000s

"We'll take another round." The man's voice cut through the background music.

It was a busy night in Seth's Cellar, the small bar in the basement of the Bullock Hotel.

Jeremy nodded toward the customer and grabbed the cinnamon whiskey bottle. "Celebrating something?" he asked.

"It's my friend's last night as a bachelor," he replied, slapping another man on the back.

A group of four men grabbed the freshly filled shot glasses, clinked them together, and threw them back.

They dropped the empty glasses on the bar before grabbing their bottles of beer and walking toward a table in the back of the room.

Jeremy gathered the glasses with one hand and wiped the counter with a rag he held in the other. The key ring jingled on his hip. He'd been tending bar at the Bullock Hotel for over a year now. The motions of serving and cleaning up were almost second nature. He surveyed the stock of beer and made a mental list of what they were low on.

"I'm heading back to restock cans and bottles," he said to Sarah, the other bartender.

Jeremy let the door shut behind him as he walked to the storage area near the back stairs. He was just a few feet from the stock when he realized he wasn't alone. Leaning against the wall, near the stairwell, was a tall man. His head was topped with a cowboy hat. A frock coat hit his knees. One foot was pressed against the back of the wall as he propped himself against it.

There shouldn't have been anyone else back there—let alone anyone dressed in full cowboy garb. But Jeremy understood immediately: This wasn't a man off the street; it was the ghost of Seth Bullock.

The air around him seemed to drop 20 degrees. Gooseflesh rose on his arms as he stood rooted in place. The figure turned its head toward Jeremy and seemed to nod at him before vanishing.

Jeremy rushed back to the bar and hustled behind the counter. He pulled the key ring from his belt loop and dropped it on the counter in front of Sarah.

"I quit," he announced.

"What?" she asked, her voice thick with surprise.

"I saw him back there again."

"Who?"

"Seth Bullock," Jeremy replied, matter-of-factly.

He'd had several encounters with the spirit over the last year. Sometimes it was just a feeling, like a person hovering over him while he took his breaks. Other times, glasses had been flung off the counter by unseen hands. He'd even heard his name spoken into his ear when no one was near him.

He added, "I've had enough with ghosts freaking me out when I come in to work. I'm done." Jeremy marched outside, never to return.

He wasn't the only employee to complain about a ghostly presence. It seems that Seth continues to make sure the hotel runs properly. Staff and guests alike report encounters with his spirit—and those of a young boy and girl. They are said to haunt the basement, which was used as a makeshift children's hospital during an outbreak of cholera and yellow fever.

With historic charm and an abundance of ghosts, the Bullock Hotel remains a popular destination. There, paranormal enthusiasts can seek proof that death doesn't mean the end of being. After all, Seth seems more than happy to provide the evidence they're looking for.

Virgil Earp

Crystal Palace Saloon
(Tombstone, Arizona)

On December 1, 1879, newly appointed deputy US marshal Virgil Earp rode into Tombstone, Arizona, alongside his two brothers Wyatt and Morgan. Virgil knew there would be plenty of opportunities to make money by enforcing the law in the booming silver-mining town. The brothers quickly realized they had their work cut out for them. Outlaws felt entitled to do whatever they wanted.

Less than two years after arriving, Virgil narrowed his law enforcement focus from federal to local when he was appointed the marshal of Tombstone. His brothers acted as his deputies. That same year, the Earp brothers, along with Doc Holliday, engaged in a shootout that would go down as one of the most famous in history when they confronted a band of outlaws in a narrow lot behind the O.K. Corral.

October 27, 1881

Ruben Coleman spoke quickly, his blood pressure spiked by worry. "I saw the Clanton brothers and McLaury brothers at Dunbar's corral. They've got guns and were talking about killing you and your brothers. They were headed to the West End Corral."

Marshal Virgil Earp listened very quietly, taking in the information.

"It's your duty to go and disarm them boys," Ruben added.

Virgil's jaw set as he stepped into the street, his hand on the pistol in his holster. Wyatt and Morgan, along with their friend Doc Holliday, joined him.

"Virgil, don't go down there, or they will murder you," Sheriff Johnny Behan called.

"Those men have made their threats, and I will not arrest them, but I will kill them on sight," Virgil replied.

The lawmen had issued an ordinance in Tombstone that anyone entering the town had to leave their weapons at the livery. They hoped it would reduce the number of gunfights that broke out on the streets, but it served to infuriate the local outlaws. Now Ike and Billy Clanton and Tom and Frank McLaury, along with Billy Claiborne, were not only breaking the law but also threatening to kill the men tasked with enforcing it.

When the lawmen saw the outlaws, Virgil gave a stern order. "Throw up your hands. I want your guns."

Instead of abiding by the order, the men drew their weapons. The air quickly filled with black gun smoke. The shootout lasted 30 seconds, with as many bullets fired, and left everyone shot except Wyatt. Ike Clanton snuck off before the shooting began, so he wasn't hurt either. Virgil, Morgan, and Doc suffered injuries they would recover from. Billy Clanton, along with Tom and Frank McLaury, were killed.

The battle left the Earp brothers marked for retribution. Two months later, Virgil was shot in the back while walking across Fifth Street. The three shotgun blasts he sustained left his right arm lame for the remainder of his life.

Just three months after that brazen attack, Morgan Earp was murdered by Ike Clanton and four of his friends while playing pool at Campbell and Hatch's Saloon. The Earp brothers left Tombstone to bring Morgan's body to Colton, California, for burial. Virgil settled there for a period of time to focus on recovering from his injures. Wyatt, on the other hand, was bent on justice. He assembled a posse and set out on a mission to avenge his brother's death in what would become known as the Earp Vendetta Ride.

Although Virgil and Wyatt ultimately left Tombstone behind after Morgan's murder, it seems that their legend remains in the infamous Wild West town.

* * *

Crystal Palace Saloon
Late 2010s

"Waitress," the man hollered at Jane as she filled water glasses a few tables away. He chugged his beer and slammed the glass down. "Bring me another, sweetheart."

Jane rolled her eyes. She'd had about enough of this guy. He'd brushed his hand against her thigh each time she brought something to him. They didn't pay her enough to put up with this.

"I've got this one," Ryan said, stepping from behind the bar with a fresh glass of beer.

"Thank you." Jane couldn't suppress the sigh of relief that followed her words.

The man grumbled a complaint about Ryan being less sexy than the waitress. He took a few long sips of the fresh beer, then excused himself. "I need to take a wiz," he said to his companions before walking to the restroom.

"We'll keep an eye on your beer, Neal," one of men at his table said with a wink. "We'll make sure no one walks by and swipes it."

After taking care of his business, Neal stood at the sink, lathering soap on his hands. The light flipped off, then back on again. Startled, he glanced around, expecting to see someone standing by the light switch. No one was there.

"Probably just old wiring," he said to himself, but he had a sudden, uneasy feeling that he wasn't alone.

He glanced into the mirror and saw a tall, thin man with a flat-brimmed cowboy hat standing behind him. The cowboy's piercing eyes glared at Neal.

Neal jumped and spun to face the angry cowboy . . . but the space behind him was completely empty.

He felt pressure on his shoulder, as if an unseen hand had grabbed him. Neal's heart pounded in his chest. He couldn't understand what was happening. It felt as if he had to push past a tall figure as he hurried to the door.

Jane watched as the man rushed to his table, spoke emphatically to his friends, then sat down clumsily in his chair and took a swig from his beer. His friends looked over his shoulder toward the bathroom and laughed.

A few minutes later, Jane took the bill to their table.

"I'll take that," Neal said, his voice less boisterous than before. He uncharacteristically kept his hands to himself as he fumbled with his wallet.

"Does anyone ever complain about the bathroom being haunted?" his friend asked with a smirk.

"All the time," Jane replied matter-of-factly.

Neal's expression told her that he was relieved to hear her words.

"I saw . . ." he started.

"A tall man dressed like a cowboy?" she asked. "People around here think it's the spirit of Virgil Earp. He had an office upstairs back when he was the marshal of Tombstone. They say he's still keeping law and order around here." Jane watched as the color drained from Neal's face. "He doesn't like people being disorderly or rude to the staff."

Neal swallowed and handed Jane cash. "Keep the change," he said. "Sorry for being a pain."

The Crystal Palace Saloon isn't the only place where people believe they can see Virgil's ghost. There have been reports of a man in a long black frock duster crossing Fifth Street in the area where Virgil was shot. The apparition always disappears before making it to the other side.

Still others believe they've seen the spirits of the men—including a tall, thin apparition in a flat-brimmed hat, believed to be Virgil—involved in the infamous gunfight outside the O.K. Corral. Although he didn't die in Tombstone, his spirit has perhaps returned to the town he worked so hard to protect.

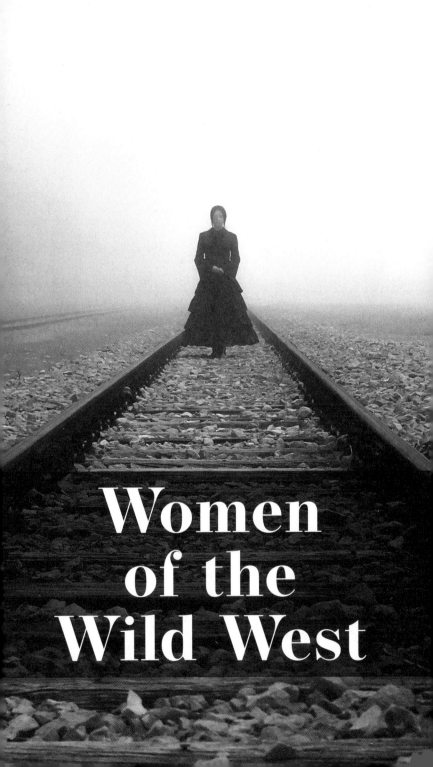

Women
of the
Wild West

Maggie Broadwater
The Fairmont Hotel
(Deadwood, South Dakota)

August 28, 1907

By the age of 21, Margaret "Maggie" Broadwater had already lived through a lot. She lost her father before she was 13 and her mother before her 16th birthday. She and her younger siblings were taken in by her uncle, but Maggie had a passion for life and wanted to see the world. She left her uncle's home around the age of 19 in search of something more.

As a young woman in the early 20th century, Maggie had limited options for earning an income. When times got tough, the girl who'd been remembered in the *Aspen Daily Times* as "one of the prettiest girls in this section of the state" and who was "beloved by all who knew her," did what she had to do to survive. While working in a house of ill repute in Thermopolis, Wyoming, she fell in love with a customer who promised to marry her. When the relationship fell apart, Maggie left Wyoming for Deadwood, South Dakota, and found work at the brothel in the Fairmont Hotel.

Now, she sat at the small vanity in her room on the third floor and glanced around the small space. She raised the tumbler to her trembling lips. Tears dropped from her cheeks, creating small ripples in the whiskey. Her shoulders shook against sobs, as she felt the liquid burn the back of her throat—a sensation she craved more each day.

This wasn't what she envisioned when she set off with a heart full of hope and dreams of a better life. She'd been gone from her family for two years, yet the quiet boredom of her uncle's home felt like a lifetime ago. She longed for that life but knew she could never go back. She believed that she was a soiled dove now—a disgrace to her parents' memory. What would her mother think if she saw her now? Maggie felt certain that her mother could never love the woman she'd become. Even the man who promised to love her forever couldn't.

As she threw back the rest of her whiskey, she thought, "No one will ever really love me."

Maggie looked at her reflection in the dusty mirror in front of her. She hardly recognized herself. She looked tired and broken. By conventional standards, she was still beautiful. Her hair was long and flowing, her skin soft and free of blemishes. But her eyes had no shine anymore. She was hollow—her soul had been drained by every calloused hand that had ever touched her.

She walked to the open window of her room and gazed into the street. A gentle breeze blew loose strands of hair away from her wet cheeks. She breathed in. There was nothing fresh about the air of Deadwood.

Maggie stepped onto the sill and turned to face the interior of her room. She took one last look at her reflection in that dingy mirror. For a moment, she imagined the girl she used to be looking back at her. Closing her eyes, she let herself fall backward.

Maggie's wrist, ribs, and jaw were broken in the fall. For a moment, the doctor was hopeful that she might survive, but the impact ruptured a kidney and left her liver severely lacerated. For two days, Maggie suffered from the terrible pain of her internal injuries, until she finally closed her eyes one last time. Her pain and shame were left behind in a body that would go unclaimed by her family.

Just two years after setting out for adventure, Maggie was gone, her body left to rot in a simple wooden box in an unmarked grave in Mount Mariah Cemetery. But if Maggie sought peace in ending her life, it seems that she failed to find it.

* * *

1995

Ron locked the door to his room and flipped off the lamp before crawling into bed and pulling up the covers. He'd purchased the Fairmont Hotel with big hopes: He planned to restore it to its former glory and rent out the rooms to guests.

Rebuilt in 1898 after a fire destroyed much of the town, the three-story structure originally featured a popular Turkish bath on the main level with a brothel on the upper floors. The hotel attracted a diverse crowd. Gold miners and cowboys frequented the top floors while prominent citizens, like lawman and local businessman Seth Bullock, visited the Turkish bath.

Ron understood that the hotel had a few lingering ghostly guests. He'd seen these spirits himself over the years: a cowboy with a long duster jacket who wandered around the first floor, the apparition of an older woman who peeked over the second-floor banister, and shadow figures—not to mention objects being moved, footsteps, doors opening and closing on their own. There was no doubt that this hotel was haunted. Ron had made peace with that and had been living on the third floor for the past five years while he worked on renovations.

He put any thoughts of ghosts out of his mind as he settled in for the night, yet something startled him awake.

Maybe it was a sound or perhaps just a sixth sense that told him he wasn't alone. Whatever it was that drew him out of sleep, he shot straight up in bed, his heart racing as if he were frightened. But he wasn't sure why.

Until he saw her.

She was tall—maybe 5 feet, 8 inches—and thin. Her long red hair hung loosely over her shoulders, a striking sight against the green silk of her dress. She was as solid as any living person, and she was staring right at him.

The door behind her was still shut and locked, so there was no way a living person could have walked in. That meant one thing: She wasn't living.

Ron wanted to jump out of the bed and run, but he was frozen. Even his voice seemed trapped inside his throat. All he could do was stare with a mix of horror and awe.

The woman watched him for about 5 minutes before vanishing. That might have been the most startling moment: the way she appeared so alive—blinking, breathing, contemplating him—and then, poof, she was gone.

Ron knew the stories of the young woman named Maggie. He wasn't sure which room had been hers, but she had lived and suffered here. In a flurry of heartache, she had decided to end her life.

Ron was left with a lot of questions, but one question had been answered: Would he continue to live in his beloved hotel? The answer was no. He could coexist with the spirits during the day but not at night. He would remain haunted by the experience and would wonder why she had chosen to reveal herself. What did she want from him that night, and would her troubled soul ever find peace? It was a cruel twist of fate that her soul should be stuck in a brothel—forever a soiled dove caught in a lifestyle that led to her demise.

Alice Walpole

Fort Davis National Historic Site (Fort Davis, Texas)

Spring 1860

Nestled in the shadows of the beautiful Davis Mountains, Fort Davis was built as a safe shelter for those traveling along the Chihuahua Trail through Texas. It was a tumultuous period of Western expansion, when proud Indigenous peoples fought to retain their land and culture, while settlers and merchants pushed toward the promise of gold and a better life.

This was hostile territory, and danger lurked within the natural charm of the grassland surrounded by ridges, green with brush and trees. The men stationed here understood the dangers all too well—and though they were glad to have their families with them, they couldn't help but worry for their safety.

Alice Walpole was a young bride when her husband, a lieutenant, was sent to Fort Davis. They left their home in Alabama and traveled more than 1,000 miles to a place that felt more foreign to Alice than anywhere she'd been before. Overcome by homesickness, Alice was desperate to bring a sense of familiarity to her quarters.

Hoping to find white roses, her favorite flower, Alice put on her blue cloak and went for a walk on the outskirts of the fort. It was a choice that would mar the fort with a tragedy—one that would be carried through legend more than a century and a half later.

Alice never returned, and despite the men's best efforts, her body was never found. It was as if she had simply vanished with the setting sun. Given the tensions that had mounted between the white settlers and the Indigenous people, it was largely presumed that Alice had become another victim in the clash between two cultures.

* * *

Several Days Later

The soldier walked quietly along the dirt path between the rows of officers' quarters. Dusk had taken hold, leaving the young man with only the moon to light the way to his barracks. The night was calm with just a light breeze whispering through the canyon.

The young soldier's path was empty, except for a woman walking toward him. Her blue cape billowed gently in the breeze as she passed.

"Good evening, ma'am," he said politely.

"Hello," he thought he heard her reply. Her voice was more like a sigh—soft and light—almost as if it had come from outside of her rather than from within.

The hair on the back of the soldier's neck spiked, as gooseflesh prickled his arms. Something about her didn't seem right.

He turned to look at her. Her steps were oddly smooth, as if she floated. The soldier followed her—and began to realize that he recognized her.

"Alice?" He spoke her name almost to himself but loud enough to be heard.

The woman seemed not to notice; she continued down the path. She rounded a corner, toward the quarters where the wives frequently gathered.

He was just a few steps behind her, yet as he made the turn, he found the path completely empty. There was no doubt in his mind of what he'd seen. Alice had returned to the fort—or at least her spirit had.

The specter of the beautiful young woman would be seen many times over the decades to come, but more than just sightings of her apparition were reported by the fort's soldiers and visitors. An inexplicable scent of roses was often noticed. Some even claimed that white roses were randomly left around the fort without explanation.

Today, visitors can tour Fort Davis State Park, and its buildings are being restored throughout the valley. The curious can explore the barracks and the fort's hospital or hike the surrounding trails. And if visitors are lucky, they might even glimpse Alice, still searching for something to ease the ache of homesickness.

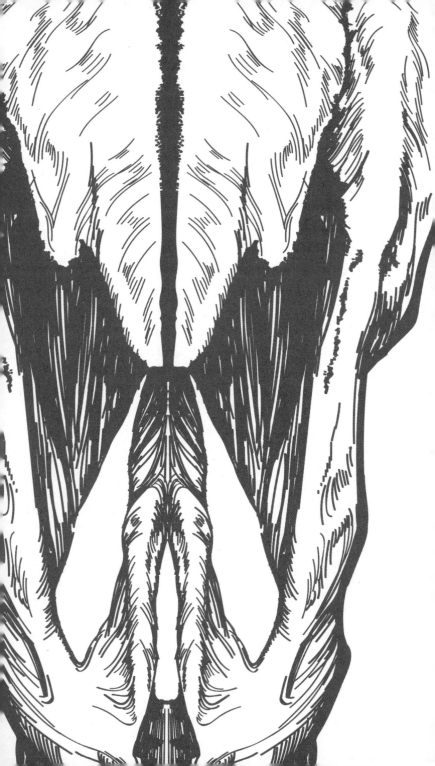

Belle Starr

The forest outside of Younger's Bend, Oklahoma

Myra Maybelle Shirley was welcomed into a well-off middle-class family in Missouri in 1848. Belle's father owned a hotel in Carthage. She was educated in the classics and studied piano. Her comfortable life was upended by the Civil War. Her father lost his business, and her brother lost his life. Devastated, the family moved to Texas to start over.

In 1866, Belle met the notorious bank-and-train robber Cole Younger. Not long after, she married Jim Reed, another outlaw. However, her daughter, Pearl, might have been fathered by Cole. Belle and Jim Reed stole money, horses, and cattle, and Belle became known as the Bandit Queen.

In 1874, Jim Reed was killed by a member of his own gang, leaving Belle free to start a gang of her own in Oklahoma. This is where she met Sam Starr, a member of the Cherokee tribe, whom she married.

For the next 10 years, they were partners in life and in crime, stealing horses and cows, until they were finally arrested. After serving five months in prison, they returned to their life of crime, until Sam was killed in a gunfight in 1886.

Belle moved on to a new partner, Jim July, a Creek man who was 15 years younger than she. In 1889, Jim July was arrested and summoned to face charges in Arkansas. Belle began the journey with him but made the decision to turn back.

Not far from the Canadian River, Belle was ambushed and shot twice in the back with a shotgun. Her murder was never solved, and her murderer was never brought to justice.

* * *

In the summer of 1970, a man named A. J. Robinson came forward with a story his grandmother, Nanna Devena, had once told him. A widowed neighbor of Belle Starr, Mrs. Devena had been feuding with some other neighbors. Back in 1889, Mrs. Devena had been attacked on her own property and beaten by one of the neighbor's boys.

In a time when the idea of "kill or be killed" was legitimately accepted, Mrs. Devena retrieved her muzzleloader and spotted her attacker, riding his horse into town. She settled in a hiding spot, waiting for his return. When she saw a rider, wearing a wide-brimmed hat, coming from town, she took aim and shot.

The next day, Belle Starr was found dead in the road.

Belle is buried near Younger's Bend, Oklahoma, and her tombstone features a carving of her favorite horse, Venus.

* * *

Younger's Bend, Oklahoma
Summer 1890

The two brothers walked through the forest in silence, keeping their footfalls light. The rumbling of the Canadian River and the night creatures chirping their summer chorus could have been soothing if the boys didn't have a job to do.

The full moon shone brightly, lighting their path and making it a great night to hunt for opossum. They quickly found what they were looking for. The silvery white hide of their prey glimmered in the moonlight. Without a word, Edward scrambled after it.

Charles watched, amazed, as his little brother chased the opossum up a tree. At just 10 years old, the kid had no fear—which came in handy when they teamed up to provide food for their family and fur they could sell. Charles could almost taste his mother's rich opossum stew, and his stomach growled in agreement.

He pulled a burlap sack from his satchel. "Okay, shake it down," he whispered.

Edward did as he was told. With all of his might, he leaned on the branch in front of him.

Shake, shake, shake.

The tree branch bounced, sending leaves and sticks rattling to the ground—and the opossum with them.

Charles was ready. The moment the creature fell to the ground, he scooped it up in his sack and tied it with a piece of twine.

Edward jumped to the ground, a smile beaming across his face. "We got one!" he announced proudly.

"We sure did," said Charles, patting his little brother on the back. "You did great."

The boys continued along the river. After several minutes, the sound of galloping horse hooves tore through the midsummer night.

"What's that?" asked Edward.

"I don't know," said Charles, trying to keep the fear out of his voice. "No one should be out riding at this time of night."

"There isn't even a road around here," his little brother added.

As suddenly as they had begun, the galloping hoofbeats ceased. Their absence somehow seemed even more alarming.

Then the boys heard a woman singing. They looked at each other, eyes wide.

"Do you think that's . . ." asked Edward.

"Belle Starr," whispered Charles.

They'd heard stories. The Bandit Queen was rumored to haunt the woods where she'd been gunned down.

"People say they've seen her ride her favorite horse, Venus, down the mountain from her grave," added Charles.

"Do you think she's still protecting her gold?" whispered Edward.

Rumors claimed that she'd buried her treasures somewhere nearby.

"Maybe she's out here hunting for her killer," Charles suggested.

"Or the killer of her horse," said Edward with a scowl. He'd been upset when he learned that Belle's favorite horse was killed in a shootout.

"Should we go?" asked Charles, feeling less afraid than he'd been before. He found it hard to be scared when the woman's song was so beautiful.

"I dunno," said Edward. "I think we should find one more opossum."

"Yeah, let's do it," said Charles, following his brother into the night.

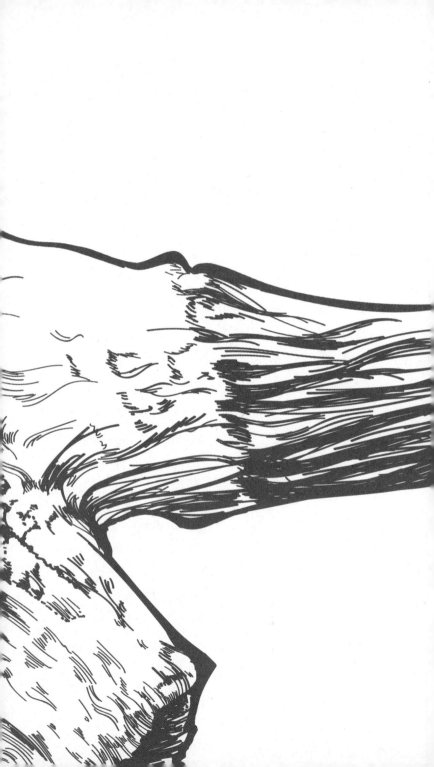

Rose—The Lady in Red

Mizpah Hotel
(Tonopah, Nevada)

In 1849, gold was found in a stream near what is now Dayton, Nevada (then part of the Utah Territory). The discovery made it a destination for 49ers. By 1852, the Gold Rush had peaked, and by 1860, it was all but over, leaving the mines depleted.

Silver became the area's new mining treasure, after the discovery of the Comstock Lode in 1859. Two years later, in 1861, Nevada became its own territory. It became a state in 1864.

* * *

Spring 1900

Jim Butler walked along the creek, looking for his mule. "That damn creature is going to be the death of me," he muttered under his breath.

This wasn't the first time it had wandered away, and it probably wouldn't be the last—unless he did a better job of tying it up. He scolded himself, then dismissed the thought.

It wasn't long before he found the mule next to an outcropping by the creek. It stood with its eyes closed, a ray of sunshine beaming down on it.

"Wouldn't we all like to take a nap in the sun?" he grumbled at the creature.

The mule opened an eye, glanced at him, and promptly closed it again.

"Come on. Back to work, like the rest of us," he said to the beast.

He reached for its rope. The mule gave a snort and dug its hooves into the earth.

Jim sighed and looked away, exasperated. It was then that he noticed the rocks that had crumbled away from the ledge. Putting off the stubborn mule for a minute, he walked over and kicked at the loose rocks. After all, the 45-year-old Californian had grown up with the knowledge that sometimes rocks held secrets. He picked up a handful and pocketed them. He couldn't say how he knew, but deep in his gut, he knew that he'd found something worth keeping.

Back home, Jim's wife, Belle, had to encourage him to return and stake a claim. That prompted the discovery of the second largest silver stake in Nevada. From it, the boom town of Tonopah was born. Soon, there were saloons, a post office, restaurants, hotels, and all the professionals needed—like doctors, lawyers, and assayers.

One of those businesses was the Mizpah Hotel, still in operation today. It opened its doors in November 1908, promising the finest amenities that included both cold and hot water, as well as the first electric elevator in the state. From its sparkling stained-glass windows to private bathrooms in every room, the hotel offered much more to weary travelers than most mining towns could.

It also housed what would become the legendary Lady in Red.

* * *

February 3, 2022

Isaac walked into the lobby at the Mizpah Hotel and was instantly glad that he opted for the historic place. The decor was authentic, and the lobby saloon looked inviting.

When he told his sister where he'd be staying, she had talked about the Lady in Red, one of the most famous ghosts in all of Nevada. Isaac wasn't sure he believed in ghosts, so none of that mattered to him.

He carried his suitcase to Room 502, tossed his jacket on the bed, and returned to the lobby bar. After a quick dinner, he went up to his room. Standing in the doorway, he tried to figure out what was off, and then he noticed: His jacket was now hanging over the back of the desk chair. Not wanting to think about what it could mean, he dismissed it as his own faulty memory.

With a job interview the next morning, Isaac got to bed at a decent time. He awoke an hour before his alarm would go off. Keeping his eyes closed, he tried to remember his dream. There was a woman whose hair had been loosely tied behind her head, and she was wearing a long red dress. Walking ahead of him, she turned and beckoned him down the hallway.

"Come with me," she whispered. "I want to show you something."

Now awake, shivers danced across his neck as if someone—or something—had touched him. He sat up straight. The hair on his arms was standing on end. A chilly draft had overtaken his room. He'd been awake; the voice had been next to him.

He lay back down to collect his thoughts. Turning to his side, he slid his hand under his pillow. It touched something small and round: a pearl.

There were dozens of possible explanations, yet it freaked him out a bit. He hurried to get ready and get out of that room. Before he left, he slipped the pearl into his pocket.

He reached the lobby at about 6:30 a.m., well ahead of schedule. Isaac rolled his suitcase into the café to find breakfast.

Seated at a table in the center of the room, he laughed at himself for getting so worked up over a dream.

A waitress filled his coffee cup and said, "You're checking out early."

"It was an interesting night," he replied. "This morning, I was alone in Room 502, but I could've sworn I heard a woman's voice in there with me."

"Room 502?" she asked with a smile. "That's just Rose, the Lady in Red. She was a lady of the night—but very high-class. She lived on the top floor. One day, she was found murdered in her room, stabbed and strangled."

Isaac leaned forward. "Who killed her?"

"Probably an ex-lover. Did she leave you a pearl?"

Isaac gaped at the waitress. "How did you know?"

She winked at him. "It means she likes you."

Isaac couldn't wait to tell his sister. He slipped the pearl out of his pocket and rolled it between his fingers. Maybe the pearl was lucky. He decided that it was a good sign—and a good day for a job interview.

Elizabeth "Baby Doe" Tabor
Matchless Mine Cabin (Leadville, Colorado)

In 1850, Horace Tabor and his wife, Augusta, arrived in Leadville with their baby. When his claim proved to be unprofitable, he turned his efforts toward running a shop alongside his wife. He also became a grubstaker, letting others use his tools for a share of their claim. One of these claims struck silver and launched his family into wealth.

Horace and Augusta disagreed about spending. While Augusta wanted to save and invest, Horace spent lavishly and generously. He funded hospitals and schools and even built the Tabor Opera House at a time when supplies still traveled through the mountains via wagons and pack mules.

Horace's path would soon converge with a woman named Elizabeth McCourt. In 1877, she and her husband, Harvey Doe, moved to Central City, Colorado, in search of a better life. Unfortunately, Harvey preferred drinking. Elizabeth, going by her nickname "Baby Doe," which was given to her because of her silky blond curls and good looks, divorced Harvey and moved to Leadville.

Now a millionaire known as the "Silver King," Horace became infatuated with Baby Doe, who was 24 years younger than him. They began a not-so-discreet affair, humiliating Augusta. Her humiliation was furthered when Horace filed for divorce without telling her.

Horace, who was filling a vacancy in the Senate, married Baby Doe in a lavish wedding that included invitations printed on silver. No other wives attended the wedding out of respect for Augusta and in protest of the scandal.

In 1893, the bottom fell out of the silver market. Baby Doe and Horace lost everything. Augusta, who had diversified her investments in companies like the Singer Sewing Company, had become a millionaire in her own right. She offered to help her ex-husband and Baby Doe, but they refused.

Most expected Baby Doe to leave the former Silver King, but she stood by his side. They sold their belongings and retreated to the mines to search for fortune once more.

Horace died in 1899, and Baby Doe, at just 38 years old, became a hermit. She guarded her miner's shack (which had once been a tool shed at the Matchless Mine) with a shotgun. She was sometimes seen around town, wearing burlap sacks on her feet because she couldn't afford shoes. Baby Doe was found frozen to death in her shack on March 7, 1935.

Now preserved as a museum, Baby Doe Tabor's cabin and the Matchless Mine allow visitors to step into history and relive the legend of the Silver King and his love.

* * *

Baby Doe's Cabin, Early 2000s

Cheryl unlocked the door and stepped into the shack that was now a museum. Every morning, she felt a sense of pride that she was helping to keep this little bit of Leadville history from being forgotten.

She straightened the "Please do not sit on me" sign on the rocking chair and smiled. People thought it was because the chair was an antique. But really, the sign was put there after several people had sat down, only to jump up because they felt as if they'd sat on someone else.

Eyeing the photos on the mantle, she found exactly what she expected. They were moved, with the photo of Augusta flipped face-down. She picked them up and held the framed photo of Baby Doe in one hand and the photo of Horace's first wife, Augusta, in the other. For a week now, she had made sure they were straightened and sitting properly next to each other— yet every morning, she'd found them moved, usually with Augusta's photo face-down.

"Okay," Cheryl said to the air, "I suppose you're right. If you don't want your photo next to Augusta's, I'll move her somewhere different."

She straightened Baby Doe's photo, now at the center of the mantel. She moved the photo of Augusta to the far corner. "Is that better?" she asked.

As if in response, a light turned on.

Ghostly occurrences aren't noticed daily at the shack, but when Baby Doe wants others to know she's around, there's no mistaking her presence. Between her spirit and the sounds of long-ago miners working in the nearby tunnels, it's clear that restless ghosts remain.

Notable Locations

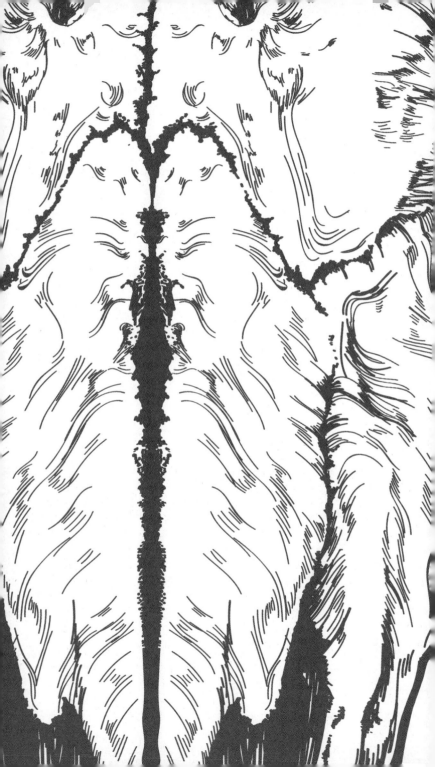

The Bird Cage Theatre
Tombstone, Arizona

The city of Tombstone took shape in the Arizona wilderness in 1877, after Ed Schieffelin discovered silver. Word spread quickly, drawing in hopeful prospectors and businessmen looking to make a buck off of the quickly booming mining community. Within just a few years, the population rose to well over 15,000 men, women, and children.

With a swinging nightlife, complete with more than 100 saloons and a world-record-setting poker game that ran continuously from 1881 to 1889, Tombstone drew some of the most famous and notorious figures in Wild West history, including Wyatt Earp, Doc Holliday, and Johnny Ringo. This blend of prominent lawmen and notorious outlaws led to one of the most famous shootouts in American West history on October 26, 1881: the Gunfight at the O.K. Corral. (See page 43.)

While ghostly apparitions have been reported throughout the city, including ghosts of the outlaws killed during the infamous shootout and restless souls buried in the notorious Boothill Graveyard, there's one haunted location that stands above the rest: the Bird Cage Theatre.

Lottie and William "Billy" Hutchinson opened the theatre on December 26, 1881, to present family-friendly shows. However, the couple quickly realized that respectable entertainment in a mining town wasn't the most economically sound plan. "Lady's Night" for the upstanding women in Tombstone quickly gave way to Cornish wrestling matches, magic shows, and comedy skits performed by men in drag. The 12 box seats, intended for prime views of the stage, were transformed into "Bird Cage Cribs," where pretty young women entertained customers.

In 1882, an article in *The New York Times* dubbed the Bird Cage Theatre as the "roughest, bawdiest, and most wicked night spot between Basin Street and the Barbary Coast."

The theatre was open for 11 years, closing in 1892 when local mining operations came to a halt. In that time, at least 26 people died within its walls from shootouts, stabbings, or suicide.

* * *

Summer 2020

Meghan stood near the open double doors at the front of the theatre, gazing across the wood-plank sidewalk into the street. A handful of tourists milled around, taking in the ambience of a Wild West town seemingly stuck in time.

Meghan turned her attention back inside the Bird Cage Theatre, where she was covering the gift shop for the afternoon.

"As you look around the building, you'll see bullet holes in the walls and ceilings," a tour guide said, leading a group into the basement to view the infamous poker table where the longest-running poker game in history was played, 24 hours a day, seven days a week, for eight years. "There are more than 120 holes throughout the building."

The Bird Cage had seen its fair share of sudden deaths. There were shootouts resulting from gambling arguments. There was the infamous murder of "Painted Lady" Margarita, who reportedly had her heart cut from her chest by a rival madam after flying into a jealous rage over her favorite customer.

As she surveyed the room, Meghan noticed movement on the catwalk above. The curtain parted, and a beautiful young woman wearing late-19th-century undergarments appeared.

Meghan understood immediately that she was witnessing something beyond explanation. She'd heard stories of people encountering full-body apparitions of women who once worked in the brothel—as if they'd stepped through a crack in time. These spirits seemed to be reliving a moment from their lives within these walls.

The woman leaned over the railing, surveying the room below, as if she were looking for her next customer. Meghan was struck by how real this apparition appeared. She wasn't a wisp or a transparent impression of a human form. She was as solid as any living, breathing person. Yet Meghan knew she wasn't.

The apparition lingered, leaning over the railing seductively for a few moments before simply vanishing. The curtain swayed lightly, the only hint that anything had been there.

Many employees and guests of the Bird Cage Theatre have reported such encounters. With so many sightings, which even include photographs, along with personal accounts of people hearing voices or being touched, there's no doubt that some spirits of the Wild West live on within the walls of this historic location. Cigar smoke still fills the air, and whiskey glasses still clink, breaking the silence of the empty theatre—as if a revelry has been caught in an ongoing loop.

Tombstone might be the most haunted town in America, and many claim that the Bird Cage is the most haunted building in town. Why do the spirits of gunslingers and ladies of the night linger? No one can know for sure. Perhaps they died so suddenly that they are not aware they've passed. Whatever the reason, the Bird Cage Theatre will hold their energy and their secrets for as long as is required.

Cerro Gordo
Ghost Town
Outside of Keeler, California

In 1865, Pablo Flores led a team of miners in search of precious metal in the Inyo Mountains. Discovering silver deposits, the men got to work—and the mining community of Cerro Gordo came to life. Soon, the small mining town was the top producer of silver in the state and had more than 4,000 people living and working there.

The Union Mine at Cerro Gordo is credited with contributing so much to the economic growth of L.A. in its early years that it's known as "the mine that built Los Angeles." This community, founded on the dreams of men seeking riches, breathed life into what is now the second-largest city in the United States.

Back then, the town was bustling with saloons, brothels, and, sadly, violence. Cerro Gordo had no law enforcement and was known for its shootouts, with a reported murder every week.

In the late 1870s, the 200-level of the mine collapsed, trapping around 35 miners. With the tunnel completely unstable and continuing to cave in, the bodies were never recovered.

Silver production peaked in the 1880s. However, the hills produced zinc, which allowed the town to carry on. But in 1938, Union Mine closed, and Cerro Gordo officially became a ghost town.

* * *

Summer 1997

Rob held tightly to the steering wheel as he maneuvered his car up the side of the mountain. It was an 8-mile trek along a rocky dirt road, devoid of guard rails to protect distracted drivers from the 8,500-foot drop to Owens Valley below.

"Oh, my," Nancy said, peering down the side of the mountain, as loose dirt from their tires rained upon the barren landscape.

They'd passed through the narrows a few minutes earlier, where the mountain seemed almost wrapped around them. Along the way, they'd already seen clues as to what was ahead—bits of mining artifacts: an old ore bin and remnants of old mining shafts—left behind by men who risked their lives to harvest the ore deep beneath the rocky terrain.

"Don't look down," Rob instructed. He was content to hug the center of the road, silently praying that they wouldn't meet any oncoming traffic. He watched for dust clouds being kicked up by an oncoming vehicle.

The newlyweds had driven more than 200 miles from their home in Los Angeles. But these last 8 miles felt like the longest stretch of the trip. The road was winding—and so bumpy that Rob's teeth rattled in his head. A few minutes back, they'd had to stop in a Joshua tree grove, just to let their car cool down.

They rolled around the last hairpin curve and started a straight upward assent. The weather-worn buildings came into sight, and they finally passed the "Welcome to Cerro Gordo" sign.

Nancy squealed with glee. "We made it!"

They met the caretaker of the ghost town, made their $99 donation, and settled into a room in the bunkhouse. Then they set out to explore the grounds, starting in the American Hotel. They were excited when the caretaker told them they were the only visitors today.

"At the time, this was considered the nicest hotel in California," Nancy said, walking through the small check-in area, into the main room.

Rob followed, the wooden floors creaking beneath his feet. "It's amazing in here," he said. "Can you imagine it full of miners, grabbing a beer after a long day in the ground?"

Nancy wandered past the bar and into a little room, where a poker table and four chairs were set up. She took another step into the room and paused.

"It feels off in here," she said.

Rob stepped into the room behind her. "What do you mean, 'off?'"

"I don't know. Heavy, I guess. That's the best way I can describe it." She walked around the small table. "I don't like it."

"We can leave," Rob noted.

"I'm so cold," she said, rubbing her hands together. Nancy stepped closer to the wall and put her finger over a hole in the wood paneling. "A bullet hole," she said. Then she glanced toward the floor where a dark stain spread across the wooden planks. "Blood," she whispered.

Rob put a hand on Nancy's shoulder. "I don't like the way this room feels either," he said, trying to ignore the skin on his arms prickling with goosebumps. "Let's get out of here."

Nancy nodded, and the couple continued their exploration of the American Hotel, soaking in the historic charm, before heading outside to explore more of the grounds. That's when they saw him: The figure of a man stood in the rear left window of the hotel. He seemed to be watching them.

"Do you see that?" Nancy asked.

"Yeah," Rob replied, taking a hold of her hand and squeezing it.

Neither took their eyes off the man. He wore a flat-brimmed hat, like someone out of an old Western movie. Then he just disappeared.

Rob looked around the property, hoping to make sense of what they'd just seen. He saw the caretaker not far away.

"Excuse me," Rob hollered, walking briskly toward him.

The caretaker nodded in acknowledgment.

"Were you just in the hotel?" Rob asked.

"Nope, been out for about an hour."

"Was someone else in the hotel?" Nancy asked.

"It's just the two of you and me here right now," he replied. Then a small smile curved his lips. "Did you see someone in there?"

Nancy replied, "Yes, a man, dressed in old-looking clothes, watching us from a back window."

The smile widened. "You saw our friend Alphonse Benoit. He's a regular around here."

"Does he work here?" Nancy asked.

"He was a woodcutter in a neighboring camp. He was murdered here more than 100 years ago. You, my friends, just saw one of our resident ghosts."

"We saw a bullet hole and bloodstain in the poker room," Nancy said.

"There are a lot of bloodstains and bullet holes around this place," answered the caretaker. "In its heyday, there was a murder here every week—which I suppose makes for a lot of restless spirits."

* * *

Today, Cerro Gordo is owned by Brent Underwood and Jon Beir. Brent has been living there since 2020 and is working to bring the town back to life, with hopes of turning the area into a tourist destination. He creates content for social media, sharing his adventures in the ghost town, and he recently wrote a book about his personal experiences there, which debuted on *The New York Times* Best Seller list.

Sadly, on June 15, 2020, at around 2:30 a.m., Brent awoke to an explosion. He rushed outside to find a fire burning in the American Hotel. By the time the firefighters arrived, the hotel had been completely destroyed, along with two other structures. This was a historic loss. The hotel first opened on June 15, 1871, and exactly 149 years later (to the day) it burned to the ground. The fire was likely the result of old electrical wiring.

Brent was determined to rebuild the hotel. As fate would have it, he had found the original floor plans for the hotel just a week or so before the fire. With those, he was able to raise the American Hotel from the ashes, bringing rebirth to a ghost town that refuses to let go of life.

The St. James Hotel
Cimarron, New Mexico

In 1865, Henry Lambert was employed as the personal chef of President Abe Lincoln. After the president was assassinated, Henry was out of a job. In 1871, he had an opportunity to buy land in Cimarron, New Mexico, from the Maxwell Land Grant. He traveled to Cimarron, where he built a saloon and restaurant that became the Lambert Inn.

Situated on the Santa Fe Trail, Cimarron was a lawless town on the main passage that connected Missouri to Santa Fe, New Mexico. The Lambert Inn began as a restaurant and saloon. Given its location, it became a refuge for outlaws—and the site of at least 20 murders over its first decade.

In 1882, the Lambert Inn was remodeled and expanded; it reopened as the St. James Hotel. By this time, the town had grown to include four hotels, 15 saloons, a post office, and its own newspaper.

Throughout the years, the hotel boasted many notorious guests, including Billy the Kid, Wyatt Earp, Black Jack Ketchum, Annie Oakley, and Buffalo Bill Cody. In addition, Jesse James stayed there under his known alias, R. H. Howard, as did his eventual murderer, Bob Ford.

By 1901, Henry Lambert's sons had taken over ownership of the St. James Hotel. When they replaced the roof, there were more than 400 bullet holes in the ceiling above the bar. Multiple layers of thick wood kept visitors sleeping above from getting shot in their sleep. Today, 22 bullet holes can be counted in the dining room ceiling.

* * *

Fall 2020

Kathy wrinkled her nose and hoped that the man who had come to fix a leak in one of the rooms didn't notice the—

"What's that smell?" asked the plumber. "It's like my old man's cigar. You don't let people smoke in here, do you?"

"No," said Kathy. "It just happens sometimes."

She didn't explain further, and he didn't ask. She let him into the room and promised to be available if he needed her.

After almost an hour, the plumber found her. "I think I've got it figured out, but I need to get into the room next door. Is anyone staying in Room 18?"

Someone was staying in Room 18: T. J. Wright, who had been dead for more than 100 years.

She slipped the master key off its hook. "Come with me." At the top of the steps, she stopped and faced the plumber. "I'm not sure what you think about ghosts or if you've heard stories about this place, but Room 18 isn't one that we rent."

The plumber chuckled. "I don't believe in any of that."

Kathy shrugged and led him to the room. "You should know that Room 18 is occupied by Mr. T. J. Wright." She hoped that if T. J. heard her tell the story, he wouldn't get so ornery. "It is said that Mr. Wright won the hotel in a poker game, but as he walked to his room, someone shot him in the back. He stumbled into his bed and bled to death. We keep it for him and don't rent it to anyone."

She opened the room. Inside was an antique metal bed frame, a coat rack, and a rocking chair. In the corner, on top of the dresser, sat a bottle of Jack Daniels, playing cards, and a water pitcher with a basin.

The plumber surveyed the room. "I just need to check that corner behind the dresser."

"Suit yourself," said Kathy. She then went back downstairs and left him to it.

Not 10 minutes later, she heard footsteps pounding quickly down the stairs. She poked her head around the corner. The plumber was hurrying to the door with his toolbox.

"I'll send a bill!" he shouted over his shoulder.

Kathy suppressed a giggle. "I bet he believes in ghosts now."

* * *

After 152 years, the hotel closed its doors on September 16, 2024, but it was quickly reopened by new owners and continues to operate today.

Bannack Ghost Town

Bannack, Montana

August 4, 1916

It's awfully hot," 14-year-old Dorothy Dunn said, walking quickly across the smooth pebbles and soft mud along the water's edge.

Her cousin Fern waded into the pond. As Dorothy walked, her steps kicked up a light spray of water that dampened the front of her blue dress. Their friend Ruth followed, letting out a giggle as the mud squished between her toes.

The air was hot and dry that afternoon, with no wind to bring relief from the August heat. Bannack Peak rose above the horizon, into the cloudless blue sky. The landscape along the pond was lush with greenery, giving the setting a storybook feel. The girls' laughter lofted into the air, making the lazy afternoon feel a little more alive.

Dorothy's parents managed the Hotel Meade in Bannack, Montana. Originally a mining camp, Bannack cropped up along a large creek where gold miners from Colorado found what they were looking for in July 1862. They named the stream Grasshopper Creek after the many green, winged chirpers that regularly bounded among the weeds along the water's edge. It didn't take long for others to learn of the gold-rich stream, and a booming mining town was born.

Less than a year later, the population was well over 3,000, with some accounts claiming that more than 10,000 men tirelessly mined the area for gold. For a short time, Bannack served as the capital of Montana— but gold fields in other parts of the state proved to be more fruitful. Eventually, Bannack's gold was all but depleted, and the treasure hunters took their dreams of riches to other parts of the West.

While the prospectors left the area, taking with them a majority of the saloon girls and much of the lawlessness that plagued the Gold Rush town, many families who had planted roots in the community chose to stay. But when the railroad was built in the 1880s without a stop in Bannack, the population steadily declined.

* * *

Smith Paddock walked a trail not far from the old dredge site that served as the girls' wading pool. The 12-year-old boy liked to explore the open fields, thinking about the outlaws who had the run of the town in its earlier days. His favorite was Henry Plummer, the outlaw who, for a while, had served as the town's sheriff. The locals had hoped the man would protect them from lawlessness, but instead, he allegedly used his position of power to protect his band of outlaws. They were allowed to terrorize the area without fear of punishment.

It wasn't long before a group of local vigilantes rounded up Sheriff Plummer and his two deputies and hanged them, without a trial, on the very gallows the sheriff had erected to hang criminals. Smith understood how legends sometimes took on a life of their own, so he wondered if Henry Plummer had actually been guilty.

He didn't pay much attention to the giggles rising from the nearby pond—until the playful splashing became frantic and the giggles turned to outbursts of terror. Smith looked toward the pond and saw the girls' heads slipping beneath the water.

He knew right away they were in trouble. The pond was shallow along the edge, but it had been used for dredging gold, so the earth under the water could drop off into deep holes unexpectedly.

Smith rushed to the water's edge, the tall weeds along the way scratching at his cheeks. He sprinted into the shallow water and, without hesitation, dove headfirst toward the girls.

He found Fern, lifted her head above the water, and paddled back to shore.

"Help Dorothy and Ruth!" she cried.

Even before the words could leave her mouth, Smith dove back into the pond. Ruth bobbed above the water as he pushed her upward, thrusting her toward the shallows.

Fern, still trembling, waded to her and pulled her to shore.

Seeing that Ruth was safe, Smith went back again into the deep water, which had taken on a frightening stillness where Dorothy had gone under. He flailed his arms in every direction, hoping to feel Dorothy, but he only felt the water swirling around him.

Twice, he came up for air. Fern and Ruth's sobs filled his ears for a few seconds before he swam downward into the deep hole. Eyes open, he saw her long, brown hair flowing among the weeds. He grabbed her under her arms and pushed them both to the water's surface.

By the time Smith swam to the edge of the pond, Fern was returning with Dorothy's parents. They took their daughter from his arms. Their frantic words could have been a foreign language for all Smith knew. His chest burned, and it seemed as if his heart was beating in his ears—the steady thump of it so loud that it drowned out Mrs. Dunn's wails as her husband rushed toward the hotel, cradling their lifeless daughter.

Smith followed, as if in a trance, and sat on the front step of the hotel's porch. A puddle dripped around him as he listened to them frantically try to revive her. Another wave of wailing, more feral than the last, confirmed what Smith already knew: Dorothy was gone.

* * *

Hotel Meade
Summer 2021

Twelve-year-old Callie walked beside her mother through the second-floor hallway of the old hotel. It'd been about 80 years since it had last served an overnight guest, but many visitors walked through its rooms, which were preserved in a state of "arrested decay."

The yellow paint, dulled by time, cracked and peeled on the walls. Stained by a century of fingerprints, windows and doors stood framed by whitewashed boards.

Callie was excited to spend an afternoon in the old mining town. She and her mom shared a fascination with the history of the Gold Rush. Bannack, completely abandoned by the 1960s, was considered Montana's best-preserved ghost town from that era.

She couldn't explain why, but Callie found herself drawn into one of the rooms. Maybe it was the sun, shining so brightly through the window. She walked toward it, captivated by its glow through the thick coating of dust.

Her mother continued down the hallway, snapping pictures through the doorways of each room, seemingly unaware of her daughter's detour.

As Callie leaned against the windowsill, gazing into the streets of Bannack, she felt a chilled breeze behind her. She turned around, startled by the unexpected coldness. A girl, not much older than herself, stood between Callie and the door. The girl wore a blue dress, like something from another era.

"Hi," Callie said, smiling politely. She'd heard that sometimes people dressed in period clothing to set the mood.

The girl didn't reply, and her expression didn't change. Nevertheless, Callie felt the warmth of a smile in her eyes—even as the chill she felt seemed to intensify.

The girl's mouth opened, as if she were speaking, but no sound came out. It was then that Callie noticed the odd blue hue of her lips and the smell of stale, dirty water. Callie wanted to ask who she was, but she felt frozen by the sudden feeling that something was very wrong with this girl. She didn't exactly feel frightened, just unsettled.

The click of her mother's camera caused Callie to glance toward the door.

Her mother peeked around the corner and grinned. "Found you," she said playfully, stepping into the room. "I thought you were right behind me. Then I turned around and you were gone."

Callie gaped as her mother walked to the exact spot where the girl had been standing, but she was suddenly gone like a white puff of breath on a winter day—one second there and gone the next—taking the chill with her.

"What is it?" her mom asked.

"There was a girl standing where you are, like 5 seconds ago," Callie said.

Her mom glanced around the room. "I didn't see anyone, but I snapped a picture just before I came in," she said, pulling her camera toward her face. She pushed a button, prompting the last photo she'd taken to appear on the screen. Her mouth dropped open.

Callie rushed to look over her shoulder.

There, just inside the doorframe, was the long brown hair of a young girl. It was all they could see—just a glimpse of the ghost who had tried to speak to Callie. It was enough to confirm that Callie had not been alone.

Callie wasn't the first child to see the spirit of Dorothy Dunn, and she certainly wouldn't be the last. It seems that the poor girl who lost her life so unexpectedly wants to tell the children who visit Hotel

Meade something important. Unfortunately, her voice is lost in the echoes of her tragic death—her warning, whatever it might be, swallowed by the waters of the dredge pond, just beyond town, more than 100 years ago.

* * *

Dorothy's spirit is just one of many believed to haunt the famous ghost town. Some suggest that the spirit of Henry Plummer and several of the town's former residents roam the boardwalks and dusty streets of the now-abandoned community. Today, visitors can walk the streets, stay at the campgrounds, or skate on the frozen dredge pond where young Dorothy lost her life so tragically.

The Custer House
Mandan, North Dakota

Around June 26, 1876

Elizabeth "Libby" Custer stood at the window of her bedroom, looking across the open fields. A worried knot formed in her stomach. The men—led by her husband, Lieutenant Colonel George Custer—had ridden away from the fort nearly six weeks ago. Since then, she'd prayed for their safe return. The Seventh Calvary Regiment had been ordered to take a stand against the Northern Plains Tribe, who refused to be relocated onto reservations after the government rescinded the agreement to let them have the Dakota territory.

Over the years, Libby had been devoted to her husband, to the point of joining him at military camps, roughing it alongside the soldiers. She was proud to follow him anywhere.

She took a deep breath and turned away from the window. She needed to steady herself and be strong for the other wives. She ventured downstairs and prepared to greet the women who were coming for a support meeting. They drank tea in the parlor and did their best to lift one another's spirits.

When a knock came at the door, the gentle buzz of conversation abruptly stopped. Worried glances were exchanged as a soldier entered the room, his continence stoic.

"They're gone, ma'am," he said solemnly.

Libby straightened, determined to be strong for whichever women might have lost their husbands. "How many?" she asked, the knot she'd felt earlier beginning to twist painfully in her stomach.

"All of them," his voice cracked.

Libby turned to the women who'd gathered in her home. The heaviness of the news fell across the room as if raining boulders upon them. As the young man's words sunk in, a choir of moans and wails erupted within the walls of the Custer home—a cacophony of agony that shook the house to its core.

* * *

Fall 2023

It had been a long day of tours at the Custer House in Fort Abraham Lincoln State Park. The pretty summer flowers were fading away as the season shifted. Leaves on the trees were beginning to lose their green.

All the tourists had left, and Mindy did a final walk-through of the home. Rebuilt in 1989, it was an exact replica of the home shared by George Custer and his devoted wife, Libby. Thanks to Libby's detailed records of furniture purchased, the site had even been furnished accordingly. Coupled with donations from Libby's family, including George's favorite writing table, family photos, personal books and papers, as well as a collection of Libby's clothes and dishes, the home was as close to a perfect replica as modern times could get.

As Mindy approached the billiard room, the familiar sound of the balls being broken emanated from within. Mindy stepped into the room, eyeing the pool table. Everything was exactly as they'd set it up. No balls were moved from their starting position.

She smiled. The familiar sounds inside the Custer House didn't even startle her anymore. The staff had come to accept that, along with the many living visitors to the state park, the fort—and the Custer House in particular—seemed to have many ghostly visitors as well.

"I'm just making sure everything is tidied up before I leave," Mindy announced. She continued along the hallway of the second floor, checking each room as she passed.

The Custers' bed was nicely made, the coverlet smooth and straight. She stepped into the next room and gently repositioned the teddy bear neatly in the center of the bed.

She finished walking through the lower level, room by room, making sure everything was as it should be. She often felt Libby's presence, approvingly following along as tourists "oohed" and "aahed" over her lovely home. Mindy believed that Libby loved the fact that her home continued to host so many guests.

After checking each room, Mindy locked the front door behind her, crossed the wide porch, and headed for home.

* * *

The next morning, Mindy was back to unlock the house and get set up for the day. Even though she had spent the previous night making sure everything was ready, she did the same every morning. At first, she had considered it a funny thing to do, but she quickly learned why her predecessor had passed along this routine: On more than one occasion, she'd found things strangely out of place, such as rumpled bedding in the primary bedroom, as if a small figure had been lying upon it.

Upstairs, she peeked at the bed where she'd carefully straightened the teddy bear. The bear wasn't there; it was propped upon the nearby rocking horse. Mindy walked toward the bear, planning to retrieve it and return it to the bed. This mischief had become a common occurrence, one that felt like a lighthearted "hello."

As she neared the rocking horse, Mindy felt an unexpected cool breeze move around her. She paused, eyes still on the bear. The wooden horse began to rock gently.

"Well, good morning to you too," Mindy said politely. "Okay, the bear can stay there for the day."

The rocking stopped, and the temperature returned to normal. Mindy smiled and stepped out of the room, finishing her rounds.

As she made her way down the stairway, Scott walked through the front door.

"I don't know why they like to move that teddy bear," she said with a laugh.

"Again?" Scott smiled. "I think they like to let us know they're here." He was already dressed in his sergeant uniform, ready to lead tours for the day. "We'll make you proud today, Libby." He said loudly up the stairs.

Of course, they didn't know for sure that Libby had moved the teddy bear, but there had been enough reports of a woman in a black gown, standing at an upstairs window, that the staff generally accepted her as the ghost.

History remembers George Custer for his efforts to take land away from the Indigenous people and for his decisions that led to the deaths of 210 men who followed him into battle. However, to Libby, he was a hero. Mindy felt honored to help keep the history of the fort alive. She understood that Libby had also been devoted to making sure her husband's legacy lived on, long after his death. It made sense that Libby kept an eye on things now, as that complex and controversial legacy was remembered.

South Side Saloon
Dodge City, Kansas

February 1878

Rain pounded the dirt road in front of the boardwalk, making tiny rivers of mud run in the wagon ruts. Lightning flashed, brightening the night sky for a second before a thunderous boom shook the darkness.

Kinch Riley, James Dalton, and H. T. McCarty hustled through the door of the old South Side Saloon. The once-bustling business had been sitting empty for several months. Formerly owned by John McGinty and Larry Deger, the South Side Saloon served the area as both a saloon and restaurant. But shortly after John's wife died, the grieving widower said he was too frightened to be in the building. Then, one day, he disappeared.

"What do you suppose happened to him?" Kinch asked, walking slowly through the empty room that once served thirsty cowboys and railroad men.

"No one saw him leave town," James replied. "In a busy place like Dodge City, you'd think someone would notice him getting on the train or heading out on horseback."

"Maybe the ghost of his missus carried him off," H. T. said with a snort.

Kinch hoped that no one noticed him shiver at the thought.

"Maybe he's hiding in the attic—hanging out for months with the bats and mice," James joked.

Kinch laughed a little too enthusiastically. He'd heard the stories of John's terror of this place after his wife passed. His sudden disappearance only amplified an already creepy situation. Larry, John's business partner, had tried to keep the place alive, but no one wanted to unwind in a haunted saloon.

"Maybe we should go next door to the Great Western Hotel for the night," Kinch suggested.

"Why pay for a room when we've got plenty here?" H. T. asked.

Kinch nodded. Renting a room would be expensive, and none of them had extra money to spare.

Dodge City was one of the roughest towns around. With gunfights and murders happening almost daily, it had gained the reputation as the "wickedest little city in the West." These men had navigated here without incident, and there was no sense in going back into the streets, in the rain, tipsy on whiskey. H. T. was right; they should sleep here.

The three men settled in on furniture left behind by John. It wasn't long before they were asleep.

Two hours into their slumber, James was awakened by bony fingers stroking his face. Startled, he opened his eyes and was shocked by a strange brightness in the room. He sat up . . . and came face to face with a woman in a white gown, standing beside him, gazing at him with a blank stare.

"What do you want?" he asked, his voice trembling.

Gooseflesh rose on the back of his arms, as the odd figure waved skeletal hands in the air, as one might do when speaking; however, no sounds were made.

Kinch rolled over where he slept, awoken by James's voice. He saw the strange glow and the woman in white, hovering over his friend. Kinch's heart raced, but his body felt frozen. It wasn't until James jumped up and leapt through a nearby window that Kinch's body finally cooperated with the voice in his head that screamed for him to run. He followed James and landed in the street beside him.

At the time of this ghostly encounter, Dodge City had been around for less than six years. With so many men losing their lives, it's no surprise the town would be haunted. One might expect to encounter the spirit of a murdered cowboy, who died so quickly that he didn't realize he was gone—not the ghost of a saloon owner's wife. But ghosts are rarely what we expect them to be.

Today, Dodge City offers haunted taxi tours that take curiosity-seekers through the historic town, where cattle wranglers and outlaws once brought lawlessness to the streets. Boothill Cemetery is a noteworthy paranormal hotspot, and the haunted Santa Fe Trail also passes through town.

The Colorado Grande Casino & Hotel
Cripple Creek, Colorado

The area around the western edge of Pikes Peak was first settled by ranchers. With the mountain rising in the distance, the lush rolling hills were a picturesque place to homestead and raise cattle. However, beneath the surface of the pastures, a golden treasure hid, waiting to be discovered.

Robert Womack, the son of a local rancher, filed a claim in 1886, when his dream of finding gold became a reality. By 1891, a small community had cropped up around one of the larger ranches. Two years later, the town, which came to be known as Cripple Creek, was the epicenter of a booming mining district. This mining community was like so many others of that time: riddled with lawlessness, bloody battles, and murder.

In the heart of the town, a grand, three-story hotel saw its share of history. Built after the fire of 1896, the redbrick structure stood through the gold boom, when the population soared past 50,000; the bloody union strike of 1903 that resulted in the deaths of at least 30 men and the imprisonment of hundreds of others; and years of quiet decline, when Cripple Creek nearly became a ghost town in the late 1980s.

Gambling and tourism brought life back to the community in 1991. The Colorado Grande Casino and Hotel was established in the historic building that has served as home to a variety of businesses over the past 100-plus years.

* * *

Winter 1968

The sun had dipped below the horizon. Katherine made her way down the hallway on the second floor, which currently held the local Masonic Lodge ballroom and several medical offices. The bustle of locals walking to and from appointments had passed, and Katherine was ready to lock up the building for the evening.

After checking that each business had turned off their lights and shut up their suites, Katherine headed for the front of the building. She was startled to hear footsteps above her. The noise was soft, like the clip of dainty feet in high heels.

"No one should be here," she said to herself.

Katherine hurried toward the staircase. Rounding the banister, she started up the steps but froze when she saw a young woman on the third-floor landing.

"Hello?" Katherine called out.

Her brow furrowed as the woman looked back at her. She appeared to be around 25 years old. Her red hair was piled loosely on top of her head, a few curls dangling below her hairline. She wore a white shirt tucked neatly into a high-waisted cotton skirt, which ended just above the top of her heeled boots. It was as if the woman had stepped through a crack in time from the turn of the 20th century.

"Maggie." The name came across Katherine's lips like a whisper.

She stared up at the ghostly apparition with awe and a strange sense of humbled gratitude that surprised her. She'd heard the ghost stories of the young woman many times. To see her firsthand, Katherine considered it an honor, of sorts.

Katherine wasn't sure what Maggie's story was or why her spirit seemed to linger in the old building, but by all accounts, Maggie was friendly.

As Maggie's lips turned up in a gentle smile, Katherine found herself smiling back. And then she was gone. It was the first time Katherine saw Maggie, but it wouldn't be the last. For decades to come, the beautiful spectral continued to grace the historic building.

Today, at the casino and hotel, Maggie's spirit is often seen happily playing the slot machines or walking through the hotel owners' apartment on the third floor. The ghostly presence has become such a fixture of the venue that the restaurant and gambling club memberships are named after her.

With the story of her life and death lost to time, Maggie's spirit leaves us to wonder who this joyful young woman might have been. Whoever she was in life, in her afterlife she's an icon of Cripple Creek lore.

Gunslinger Gulch
Anaconda, Montana

Embedded with a deep history of mining, the area around Anaconda, Montana, has seen its share of dark times, both above- and belowground. Anaconda sits over a series of mining tunnels, where thousands of men worked tirelessly to remove copper, silver, and gold. Many of them lost their lives in mine fires, as well as shootouts.

Nestled in a small valley between rolling hills, 6 miles outside of Anaconda, sits a small Wild West ghost town. However, this motley mix of buildings from the mid- to late-1800s is not a typical ghost town. Rather, it's a collection of original buildings that were brought to the property from various Montana locations, arranged along a single main street, to go with the weather-worn, white-washed church that overlooks it all from atop a hill. Back in the 1990s, the intent of this project—known as Gunslinger Gulch—was to build a destination for history lovers to connect with the past.

The buildings that make up Gunslinger Gulch came from nearby mining communities, including Butte, less than 30 miles away. In Butte, 168 men died beneath the town in a fire that is considered one of the worst mining disasters in the history of the United States.

Gunslinger Gulch had already changed hands a few times when Karen bought it. She moved with her three children from Seattle, Washington, to embrace a new life. It wasn't long before the family realized that the old buildings offered more than rustic charm. They seemed to have stories to tell—with ghosts woven into the plot. Gunslinger Gulch was undeniably haunted.

Karen and her kids reported being touched and scratched, seeing shadow figures and full-body apparitions, and hearing disembodied voices. They captured videos of objects being moved by unseen hands. The ranch even starred in two seasons of its own TV show, in which paranormal investigators tried to understand and resolve the hauntings for Karen's family.

Today, the ranch is open to guests, with several rooms available for overnight stays. It's also available to rent for filming and as an event venue.

* * *

Winter 2019

The temperatures had dropped significantly since the sun went down, and a winter chill seemed to sweep through the gulch. Karen and her children had only been at the ranch for a couple of weeks, and Karen knew she had her work cut out for her. But there was something about this place. She felt drawn to it in a way she couldn't explain.

Her kids seemed supportive of the move—maybe even enthusiastic. As a single mom of teen and young-adult children, she was excited to share new adventures with them. Buying a ghost town could turn out to be the adventure of a lifetime.

The buildings didn't have running heat, so Karen decided to warm up in her car. In the moonlight, the buildings cast long shadows over the dusting of fresh snow. These buildings were hers. She owned a town. The thought made her smile.

Tap. Tap. Tap.

Karen was startled by the sound of someone knocking on the car. Her body tensed as she tried to decide whether she'd imagined the sound.

Tap. Tap. Tap.

Karen opened the door, stepped out of the vehicle, and looked around, worried that a stranger might be on her property. Yet as she looked around the vehicle in the snow, she saw no footprints other than her own. She was completely alone, standing in a ghost town where unseen hands were trying to get her attention.

* * *

2020

Karen's children, Chloe and her two brothers, helped their mother around the ranch. Chloe was using the restroom in the log cabin, but something about this building made her uneasy. For some reason, when she was in this space, she felt a heavy sense of sadness.

She shrugged it off. Most of the buildings had a unique energy to them, but maybe her mind was just messing with her. The buildings were all more than a century old, so it made sense they'd feel a little creepy.

She hadn't locked the bathroom door. She was alone—at least, she thought she was, until she heard two loud footsteps just outside the bathroom door. Perhaps one of her brothers had come into the cabin.

She was about to call to them, when the doorknob began to turn. Before she could fully understand what was happening, the door flung open.

Eyes wide with shock, Chloe realized that no one else was there. She ran from the bathroom and rushed out the front door, still buttoning her pants. Her heart pounded as she stood outside and looked back at the cabin she'd just fled from. At that moment, she knew that the sadness was not her imagination. Something inside those walls was angry and wanted those who entered to feel it. After that, Chloe avoided the cabin as much as she could.

* * *

Over the years, it became clear to Karen that the ranch held many secrets. Her family would come to know some of them and were content to let the others stay buried. What did they learn from it all? For one thing, it seems as though buying a ghost town might mean getting the ghosts that come with it.

The Lost Souls of the Yellow Jacket Mine

Gold Hill, Nevada
April 5, 1869

Timothy Griffin awoke with a start. The terror from his dream lingered long after he was fully awake. While he struggled to recall the details, the dream's message was clear: Enter the Yellow Jacket Mine again and die.

As a miner, Timothy hadn't chosen the easiest life. He was employed by the Yellow Jacket Mine in Gold Hill, Nevada. The Yellow Jacket was owned by robber baron William Sharon and was part of the Gold Hill Shafts that intersected with the competitor Kentuck and Crown Point mines. The shafts descended more than 1,000 feet. Collectively, the three mines had more silver wealth in the mile-and-a-half-long tunnels that ran between Gold Hill and neighboring Virginia City than all the gold wealth that had been discovered in California.

Timothy didn't have to consider his dream for long. Less than a year earlier, his cousin James had been killed with two other miners when the rope for the cage in which they had been descending into the tunnels snapped, sending the miners to instant death.

Instead of reporting to work that morning, Timothy decided to pack his things and head west to California, leaving Nevada behind.

* * *

April 7, 1869

At 7 a.m., 25 miners headed down into the mine in a Crown Point cage, past the floors that had already been mined of their minerals. Two got off at the stop for the 230-foot level, while others exited at the 600-foot stop, the 800-foot stop, and the 900-foot stop. A minute later, the cage was back at the top, and another crew began its descent.

Not far away, men from the Yellow Jacket mine were also on their way to work. Unbeknownst to them, a Yellow Jacket miner from the night shift had left a candle burning at the 800-foot level; it ignited the pine structures holding up the earth between the Yellow Jacket and Kentuck mines. The fire smoldered . . . waiting.

The methane, commonly found in underground mines, ignited with a fiery blast, and the burning wooden framework began to collapse. Smoke and carbon monoxide rushed outward, threatening anyone in their path.

Candles blew out, and men—desperate to escape—hurried to the cages, which were already full and already on their way up.

When one cage came back down, only six men managed to stumble onto it. Brothers George and Richard were among them. As the cage rose, George lost consciousness but kept a tight grip on Richard, who had fallen mostly off the edge of the cage. Richard's head was torn from his body, and his left arm was nearly detached.

By the time the cage reached the surface, George was the only one still alive. The other five riders had perished. Tragically, despite surviving his dangerous ascent, George succumbed to smoke inhalation and carbon monoxide poisoning. He, too, died.

In the end, at least 36 deaths were attributed to the fire, and there might have been more. Some of the single men, without families, may not have been reported as missing.

The fire burned for three weeks, and the incident became the deadliest mining tragedy in Nevada's history.

* * *

November 10, 1920

W. P. Bennett had spent four years in the Yellow Jacket Mine as a powder man, in charge of handling the explosives.

Pete Langan, the foreman, stopped W. P. deep within the mine. "I saw two shovels up on the 1,000-foot level. Can you get them?"

"Sure, boss," said W. P. He took his lantern and got in the cage to go up to the deserted level.

It didn't take him long to find the shovels. He picked them up and started back. But he heard a stomp against the wooden planks of the abandoned floor above him. Then another and then another. The lantern trembled in his hand as he recalled the mine's ghostly rumors.

He hurried to a nearby ladder and climbed down, dragging the shovels with him. His feet were on the bottom rung of the ladder when he heard it again.

Stomp. Stomp. Stomp.

This time, the loud footsteps were immediately above him, right where he'd been standing just a few minutes ago.

He could feel the blood draining from his face, but he found the courage to shout, "Who's there? Anybody up there?"

He knew in his soul that no one was.

The shovels that were tucked securely under his left arm suddenly flew out in front of him, as if pushed violently from behind. They hit a wall 12 feet away before clattering down the hole that housed the next ladder.

Chills rushed through his body, and his teeth began to chatter. The stomping above started again.

Stomp. Stomp. Stomp.

W. P. hurried to the ladder and then continued downward. He found the other men and asked for Pete, who must have been playing a joke on him.

"Pete has been up on the surface," said his friend Jack.

"What happened to you?" Robert asked.

"I . . . don't know," W. P. replied. "I . . . I just got sick."

"I don't believe you," said Jack.

Later, when they were all at dinner, Robert asked again, "What happened?"

W. P. shrugged. "I don't know."

"Where were you?" asked Jack.

W. P. hesitated before answering. "Boss sent me to the 1,000-foot level to pick up some shovels."

The men nodded, knowingly.

"That explains it," said Jack.

"You said the footsteps started above you? That would be the 900-foot level, where many men were lost," noted Robert.

Jack's voice became a whisper. "Their bodies have never been recovered. Some say they were walled in—behind the walls built to contain the fire."

"Men have quit because of it," said Robert. "They gave up good work because they couldn't handle the ghosts."

* * *

Gold Hill and nearby Virginia City are said to be the most haunted towns in Nevada, if not the entire country. Today, brave adventurers can rent a miner's cabin at the base of the Yellow Jacket headframe.

Bibliography

PREFACE
> No author. "Allan Pinkerton's Detective Agency."
> PBS (pbs.org). Accessed January 4, 2025.

TOM "BLACK JACK" KETCHUM *(Cimarron, NM)*
> Alexander, Kathy. "Black Jack Ketchum Lives
> On! A Ghost Story." Legends of America
> (legendsofamerica.com). November 2021,
> updated March 2025.

> Alexander, Kathy. "Train Robber – Black Jack
> Ketchum." Legends of America (legendsofamerica
> .com). Updated February 2023.

> Burton, Jeffrey. "Thomas Edward 'Black Jack'
> Ketchum." *The Seibel Family Stories* (seibelfamily
> .net). February 2002. Accessed November 1, 2021.

JESSE JAMES *(Bardstown, KY; Kearney, MO)*
> Adams, Kirby. "Old Talbott Tavern History."
> *Courier Journal* (courier-journal.com).
> October 17, 2022.

> Alexander, Kathy. "Haunted Jesse James Farm,
> Kearney, Missouri." Legends of America
> (legendsofamerica.com). Accessed January 2, 2025.

> Hometown Ghost Stories. "The Ghost of
> Jesse James: Celebrity Hauntings." YouTube
> (youtube.com). June 17, 2022.

> Nickell, Joe. "Jesse James's 'Haunts': Legends,
> History and Forensic Science." *Skeptical Inquirer*
> (skepticalinquirer.org). July/August 2016.

> No author. "Biography: Jesse James." PBS
> (pbs.org). Accessed December 13, 2024.

No author. "Ghost Encounters at the Tavern." Talbott Tavern (talbotttavern.com). Accessed January 4, 2025.

No author. "Oddities and Information." *The Oklahoman* (Oklahoman.com). May 7, 2000.

TOM HORN *(Cheyenne, WY; Boulder, CO)*
Chandler, Nathan. "The Ghost of Wild West Gunslinger Tom Horn Still Haunts Wyoming." History: How Stuff Works (history.howstuffworks.com). Accessed October 16, 2024.

Legends of the Old West. "Tom Horn, Ep. 6 - The Murder of Willie Nickell." YouTube (youtube.com). October 26, 2022.

Nickell, Joe. "The Saga of Tom Horn: Is the Hanged Man's Ghost Still at Large?" Skeptical Inquirer, Vol 43, No. 2 (skepticalinquirer.org). March/April 2019.

No author "The Hanging of Tom Horn." Eyewitness to History (eyewitnesstohistory.com). 2012.

No Author. "Topics: Johnson County War." Wyoming History Day (wyominghistoryday.org). Accessed October 16, 2024.

No author. "Willie Nickell." Find A Grave (findagrave.com). Accessed October 16, 2024.

JEAN BAPTISTE *(Salt Lake City & Antelope Island, UT)*
Adams, Andrew. "'Ghost' Island: Historic ranch leaves visitors uneasy, touched, even scratched." KSL.com (ksl.com). October 26, 2021.

Jones, Jennifer. "Jean Baptiste: Utah's Exiled Grave Robber." The Dead History (thedeadhistory.com). November 12, 2012, updated February 14, 2025.

Prettyman, Brett. "Get Your Spook On: Northern Utah's Most Haunted Places." Life Utah Elevated (visitutah.com). Accessed January 11, 2025.

Romero, Tyson. "Utah's Most Haunted: Grave robber's ghost at the great Salt Lake." ABC4 (abc4.com). October 16, 2023.

WILD BILL HICKOK *(Deadwood, SD)*

Di Certo, Joseph J. "Wild Bill Hickok: American Frontiersman." Britannica (Britannica.com). Updated March 30, 2025. Accessed November 23, 2024.

Galloway, Taraya. "'Wild Bill' Hickok's Last Hand." *Fishwrap* (blog.newspapers.com). August 2, 2016.

Garofalo Paterno, Anne (supervising producer). "Deadwood." *Ghost Lab* (Season 2: Episode 13). 2011.

No Author. "Jack McCall & the Murder of Wild Bill Hickok." *BHVisitor* (blackhillsvisitor.com). August 28, 2017.

Weirens, Michael. "Which Cards was 'Wild Bill' Hickok Holding when He was Murdered?" *True West: History of the American Frontier* (truewestmagazine.com). October 13, 2016.

SETH BULLOCK *(Deadwood, SD)*

Alexander, Kathy. "Seth Bullock – Finest Type of Frontiersman." Legends of America (legendsofamerica.com). Updated July 2023. Accessed December 7, 2024.

Bagans, Zak (executive producer). "Halloween Special: Deadwood: City of Ghosts." *Ghost Adventures* (Season 11: Episode 11). October 31, 2021.

No author. "Infamous Deadwood: Sheriff Seth Bullock." Historic Deadwood (deadwood.com). Accessed December 1, 2024.

No author. "The Legend & Restoration of Historic Bullock Properties." The Historic Bullock Hotel (historicbullock.com). Accessed December 7, 2024

Nightmare Stories. "Ghosts of Deadwood." YouTube (youtube.com). June 24, 2022.

VIRGIL EARP *(Tombstone, AZ)*

Alexander, Kathy. "Ghosts of Tombstone, Arizona." Legends of America (legendsofamerica .com). Updated November 2024/ Accessed December 7, 2024.

Alexander, Kathy. "Morgan Earp – Killed in Tombstone, Arizona." Legends of America (legendsofamerica.com). Updated November 2022. Accessed December 7, 2024.

Carr, Julie. "Tombstone, Arizona: Crystal Palace Saloon." HauntedHouses.com (hauntedhouses .com). Accessed December 7, 2024.

No Author. "The Ghosts of the OK Corral." Ghost City Tours (ghostcitytours.com). Accessed December 7, 2024.

No Author. "Virgil Earp." National Park Service (nps.gov). Accessed December 7, 2024.

MAGGIE BROADWATER *(Deadwood, SD)*

Enss, Chris. "Wild Women of the West: Madam Belle Haskell and the Demise of Maggie Broadwater." *Cowgirl* (cowgirlmagazine.com). May 10, 2023.

No Author. "Maggie Broadwater." Find A Grave (findagrave.com). Accessed November 24, 2024.

No Author. "Mary F 'Molly' Scott Broadwater." Find A Grave (findagrave.com). Accessed November 24, 2024.

Staff Writer. "Maggie Broadwater Dies." *The Daily Deadwood Pioneer-Times*. August 31, 1907.

Traegler, Rob. "Ghosts of Deadwood." *The Dead Files* (Season 4: Episode 10). January 10, 2014.

ALICE WALPOLE *(Fort Davis, TX)*

Geurkink, Lee Virden. "The Ghosts of War." Madeworthy & Tanglewood Moms (tanglewoodmoms.com). June 5, 2021. Accessed December 22, 2024.

No Author. "The Second Fort Davis: 1867–1891." National Park Service (nps.gov). Accessed December 23, 2024.

Roberts, Nancy. *Ghosts of the Wild West*. Columbia, South Carolina: University of South Carolina Press. 2008.

BELLE STARR *(Younger's Bend, OK)*

Bell, Roger. "Where the Gem Sparkles Yet: The History of the Grave of Belle Starr." *Oklahombres Journal* (oklahombres.weebly.com).

Dary, David. "The Shooting of Belle Starr." *The Oklahoman* (oklahoman.com). August 29, 1982.

Mullins, Jonita. "Ghost stories surround death of Belle Starr." *Muskogee Phoenix* (muskogeephoenix.com). October 19, 2009.

No author. "This Day in History: Belle Starr murdered in Oklahoma." History (history.com). November 16, 2009, updated January 31, 2025.

ROSE—THE LADY IN RED *(Tonopah, NV)*

Hall, Shawn. "Tonopah's History." Town of Tonopah, Nevada (tonopahnevada.com). Accessed January 18, 2025.

No author. "The Haunted Mizpah Hotel." US Ghost Adventures (usghostadventures.com). June 1, 2022.

No author. "Meet the Lady in Red Nevada's Most Famous Ghost." Travel Nevada (travelnevada.com). Accessed January 17, 2025.

Tami. "Who Is the Lady in Red?" Nevada Ghost Towns & Beyond (nvtami.com). March 12, 2023.

ELIZABETH "BABY DOE" TABOR *(Leadville, CA)*

Alexander, Kathy. "Baby Doe Tabor: Scandal in Denver." Legends of America (legendsofamerica.com). Updated March 2025. Accessed on January 18, 2025.

No author. "Leadville." Haunted Colorado (hauntedcolorado.net). Accessed January 19, 2025.

No author. "The Legacy of Horace Tabor." Leadville, Colorado (leadville.com). Accessed January 19, 2025.

No author. "Podcast: The Tabor Opera House." Atlas Obscura (atlasobscura.com). June 8, 2023.

THE BIRD CAGE THEATRE *(Tombstone, AZ)*

Belanger, Jeff (Writer), Zak Bagans and Nick Groff (director). "Bird Cage Theater." *Ghost Adventures* (Season 2: Episode 5). July 3, 2009.

No Author. "History of The Bird Cage Theater." Tombstone Bird Cage (tombstonebirdcage.com). Accessed November 3, 2024.

No Author. "The Haunted Birdcage Theatre:
Who, or what, is haunting this famous theatre?"
Ghost City Tours (ghostcitytours.com).
Accessed November 3, 2024.

CERRO GORDO GHOST TOWN
(Cerro Gordo, CA)

Fleeman, Michael. "Remote Ghost Town and Its
Apparitions Can Be Yours for $99 a Night." *Los
Angeles Times* (latimes.com). October 26, 1997.

Ghost Town Living. "Building A Hotel In
A Ghost Town (3 Year Timelapse)." YouTube
(youtube.com). January 6, 2024.

Ghost Town Living. "Top 5 Scariest Moments
at Cerro Gordo." YouTube (youtube.com).
October 31, 2021.

Ghost Town Living. "Tragedy Strikes in The Ghost
Town of Cerro Gordo." YouTube (youtube.com).
June 18, 2020.

Vargo, Cecile Page. "Cerro Gordo History."
Explore Historic California (explorehistoriccalif
.com). Accessed December 8, 2024.

THE ST. JAMES HOTEL *(Cimarron, NM)*

Alexander, Kathy. "Haunted St. James Hotel in
Cimarron, New Mexico." Legends of America
(legendsofamerica.com). Updated November 2024.

Lowth, Marcus. "The Ghosts of Room 18 at the
St. James Hotel." UFO Insight (ufoinsight.com).
January 23, 2019.

Ortega, Mikayla. "Historic St. James Hotel in
Cimarron Closes Its Doors." Questa del Rio
News (questanews.com). September 30, 2024.

No author. "St. James (Don Diego) Hotel." Santa Fe Trail Historic Sites (historic-trails.unm.edu). Accessed January 18, 2025.

No author. "Stay Where Famous Outlaws Hung Their Hats." St. James Hotel (exstjames.com). Accessed January 18, 2025.

BANNACK GHOST TOWN *(Bannack, MT)*

Alexander, Kathy. "Henry Plummer— Sheriff Meets a Noose." Legends of America (legendsofamerica.com). Updated January 2024.

Goth, Mitch. "Bannack Ghost Town." Haunted US (hauntedus.com). Accessed December 15, 2024.

No Author. "Bannack: Haunting Montana." Visit Southwest Montana (southwestmt.com). Accessed December 15, 2024.

No Author. "Bannack State Park." Montana Fish, Wildlife & Parks (fwp.mt.gov). Accessed December 15, 2024.

Staff Writer. "Boy Saves Two Girls but Another Drowns." *The Butte Miner.* August 5, 1916.

Staff Writer. "Young Girl is Drowned." *The Dillon Examiner.* August 9, 1916.

THE CUSTER HOUSE *(Mandan, ND)*

1st Infantry Division. "The Custer House: A Haunted History." YouTube (youtube.com). November 8, 2016.

Carr, Julie. "Mandan, North Dakota: Custer House." HauntedHouses.com (hauntedhouses .com). Accessed December 22, 2024.

Leah. "The Spooky Tale of the Ghosts at North Dakota's Fort Abraham Lincoln Will Give You Chills." Only In North Dakota (onlyinyourstate .com). May 20, 2020.

Staff Writer. "The Haunted History of the Custer House." KX News (kxnet.com). October 26, 2021.

Urwin, Gregory J.W. "Battle of the Little Bighorn" Britannica (britannica.com). December 20, 2024. Updated February 20, 2025.

SOUTH SIDE SALOON *(Dodge City, KS)*

Alexander, Kathy. "Dodge City, Kansas— A Wicked Little Town." Legends of America (legendsofamerica.com). Updated November 2024. Accessed December 22, 2024.

Haunted Taxi Ghost Tours, The Haunted Journey Show. "The Haunted Taxi Ghost Tours of Dodge City KS Pre-Show 2023." YouTube (youtube.com). April 20, 2023.

Legacy of the West. "Dodge City's Haunted Saloon (Ghost Stories of the Old West Episode 1)." YouTube (youtube.com). October 1, 2021.

Staff Writer. "The Haunted House." *Dodge City Times.* February 2, 1878.

THE COLORADO GRANDE CASINO & HOTEL *(Cripple Creek, CO)*

No author. "Colorado Grande Casino and Hotel." Denver Terrors (denverterrors.com). June 19, 2021. Updated November 16, 2024.

No author. "Ghosts of Cripple Creek, Colorado." Legends of America (legendsofamerica.com). Accessed December 26, 2024.

No author. "Ideas in Conflict: Opposing Views of the Cripple Creek Strike." History Matters (historymatters.gmu.edu). Accessed January 18, 2024.

Staff Writer. "The Ghosts of Cripple Creek." The *Mountain Jackpot News* (mountainjackpot.com). October 26, 2022.

GUNSLINGER GULCH *(Anaconda, MT)*

Fernandez, Neil. "Get Help." *The Ghost Town Terror* (Season 1: Episode 2). March 11, 2022.

Margolis, Josh. "Anaconda area ghost town owner seeking investment to remain open." NBC Montana (nbcmontana.com). May 1, 2024.

No Author. "Ghost Town Terror | Gunslinger Gulch." Visit Southwest Montana (southwestmt .com). Accessed January 19, 2024.

THE LOST SOULS OF THE YELLOW JACKET MINE *(Gold Hill, NV)*

Bernstein, Matthew. "Who Started the Infamous 1869 Yellow Jacket Mine Fire that Claimed Three Dozen Men?" HistoryNet (historynet.com). July 25, 2023.

Tami. "Yellow Jacket Mine Gold Hill, Nevada." Nevada Ghost Towns & Beyond (nvtami.com). May 22, 2020.

Woodyard, Chris. "The Haunted Yellow Jacket Mine." Haunted Ohio (hauntedohiobooks.com). Accessed January 14, 2025.

Young, Jennifer. "On This Day In 1869, The Unthinkable Happened in Nevada." Only In Nevada (onlyinyourstate.com). Updated January 4, 2023.

About Jessica Freeburg

essica Freeburg is an internationally published author, history nerd, and researcher of the unexplained. She has written a wide variety of books, ranging from graphic novels to paranormal fiction, as well as nonfiction focused on creepy legends and dark moments from history.

As the founder of Ghost Stories Ink, Jessica has performed paranormal investigations at reportedly haunted locations across the US. She has appeared in documentaries and shows on such networks as the Travel Channel and Amazon Prime—talking about ghosts and haunted places—and can often be heard cohosting the wildly popular podcast *Darkness Radio*.

You can learn more about Jessica's work at jessicafreeburg.com.

About Natalie Fowler

Natalie Fowler, once a practicing attorney, is now an award-winning author and ghost writer. Natalie's published works include nonfiction books on poignant—though sometimes dark—historical events and haunting legends.

She is the researcher and historian for Ghost Stories Ink and has led paranormal investigations at some of the most notoriously haunted locations in the country. Inspired by the concept of spirit rescue, she cofounded a paranormal group called Paranormal Services Cooperative and has published accounts of her work as a medium in this field. You can learn more about her work and publications at nataliefowler.com.

The Story of AdventureKEEN

We are an independent nature and outdoor activity publisher. Our founding dates back more than 40 years, guided then and now by our love of being in the woods and on the water, by our passion for reading and books, and by the sense of wonder and discovery made possible by spending time recreating outdoors in beautiful places.

It is our mission to share that wonder and fun with our readers, especially with those who haven't yet experienced all the physical and mental health benefits that nature and outdoor activity can bring.

#bewellbeoutdoors